Dramatic Narrative in Preaching

DAVID M. BROWN

MORE EFFECTIVE PREACHING SERIES

Judson Press ® Valley Forge

DRAMATIC NARRATIVE IN PREACHING

Copyright © 1981
Judson Press, Valley Forge, PA 19481

Library of Congress Cataloging in Publication Data

Brown, David M. (David Mark), 1949–
  Dramatic narrative in preaching.

  Bibliography: p.
  1. Story sermons.   2. Preaching.   I. Title.
BV4307.S7B76   251   81-8345
ISBN 0-8170-0911-6   AACR2

The name JUDSON PRESS is registered as a trademark in the U.S. Patent
Office.
Printed in the U.S.A. ⊕

This book is dedicated to the
Stelton Baptist Church of Edison, New Jersey,
which, first and last, endured narrative preaching
and encouraged me in its use.

Acknowledgments

The production of this volume is due to years of relationships with all kinds of people, along with a continuous interest in creative writing and fiction reading. My thanks extends to my dear family, many friends, teachers, innumerable writers and speakers, and scores of strangers too numerous to count.

Most significantly, however, I wish to thank three who had direct influence on the writing of this book:

Dr. Donald Macleod, who skillfully tutored and encouraged me in this project;

Mrs. Jean Scovell, who faithfully typed the manuscript while under the pressures of her regular secretarial duties; and, most importantly,

my tender and loving wife, *Ellen,* who patiently and prayerfully has been my support.

Contents

Introduction

The night was warm, and I stood in sandaled feet and a blue plaid tuxedo jacket. The crackling campfire was encircled by twenty-five or thirty young people who had gathered for a retreat in eastern Pennsylvania. It was my first experience with narrative preaching, and, in spite of my discomfort at trying out a new approach to homiletics, I quickly discovered the spellbinding effect of the first-person sermon. My rich young ruler ended his disturbing confrontation with Jesus and left the campfire circle with the words "I cannot make that kind of commitment. It's just too hard. It's just too hard." There seemed to be a troubled stirring among the young people while they sang, "I Have Decided to Follow Jesus," and later some of them told me that they had decided to give Jesus a serious chance with their lives.

Since that evening, I have learned much about the preaching narrative, mostly through trial and error, and have used this exciting style of preaching on many different occasions and most extensively in the pulpit ministry. Each time a narrative is written and presented, the excitement of the biblical message pulsates through tired veins, and then the story is alive again.

The purpose of this book is to examine the preaching narrative methodologically from its inception to its delivery. However, before the preaching narrative is pursued, there are definitions to be understood. Exactly what is a narrative? And before that is answered, since a narrative is a form of preaching, what exactly is a sermon? Those definitions will be examined, and concluding the introductory statements, the scope of this study will be covered.

The Sermon

There have been many definitions of what a sermon is. Some

of those definitions are simple: A sermon is a "word from the Lord for you."[1] Some of those definitions are more complex: A sermon "is the Word of God (Jesus Christ) who has been revealed in the pages of the written Word (the Bible) coming to the hearing of people by the proclamation of the Word (preaching)."[2] But whatever a sermon is, it involves the spoken word as it is heard by others. Certainly it has as its very foundation the Word of God revealed in the Scriptures. And that Word calls people to response and action.

A sermon, then, *is a call to action on some point of the biblical message.*

There are two considerations in this definition. The first is that a sermon finds its foundation in the biblical story—either a very select passage or verse, or some broad, thematic type of study. The framework for any sermon is to bring its hearer to some further understanding of God through Jesus Christ, of human nature, or of any other theme which is firmly rooted in the biblical message.

Second, a sermon is a call to action. A sermon goes beyond the mere teaching ministry of the pulpit (though any sermon should include teaching). The goal of preaching is not the mere impartation of factual data (however valuable that material may be). A sermon is not solely concerned with broadening one's knowledge. It is aimed at bringing people to a point of decision. It is to move them to do something about the teaching material they have received. Preaching must in some way compel people to take action on what they have heard.

Thus a sermon is a spoken presentation of some aspect of the biblical message, which calls its hearers to response.

The Narrative as Sermon

Briefly stated, *a narrative is the telling of a story.* In the case of a preaching narrative the story is a biblical one, or a biblically based one, told to enhance the biblical message, to bring it alive, to involve its listeners personally in the sharing of the Good News stories. A narrative is filled with all the elements of a good story: imagery, color, an appeal to the senses, and a direct involvement of the narrator in the events of the story. It is through the *method* of the narrative that the preaching is done.

Naturally, any sermon includes both teaching and preaching.

[1] William D. Thompson, *A Listener's Guide to Preaching* (Nashville: Abingdon Press, 1966), p. 14.
[2] *Ibid.,* p. 25.

The narrative, as a distinct style of sermon, also contains elements of both teaching and preaching. The teaching comes through background study and use of the Bible. The preaching is evident in the stated purpose toward which the narrative moves, as people are called to act on what they hear.

The preaching narrative combines sermon and story into one unit. It becomes far more than the mere telling of a story. It becomes far more than a mere sermon. It takes the best of both worlds—the excitement and attentive spirit that accompany a good story with the purpose and challenge of a sermon. The narrative itself is not just a literary device used to get across a point. It is, rather, more a spoken word, a story which has intent in its telling. (The Gospel writers worked under the same principle. See John 20:30-31.)

Narratives can take on many different forms. There may be a strictly biblical narrative (from the point of view of any biblical character—Amos, Peter, or even the beaten man in the parable of the good Samaritan). There are also nonbiblical narratives by characters who could have been eyewitnesses to some biblical happening (a stable boy at the birth of Jesus, one of the guards at the tomb, or a tax collector friend of Levi). The narrative may also take on, though less frequently, a historical character (William Carey, Russell Conwell, or a preacher at Plymouth Colony). Finally, narratives may come from contemporary situations (a farmer in his field, a street evangelist, or a young lover).

Any one of these suggested possibilities may be a seed for a good story, but that does not make it automatically good narrative material. The point at which such a story becomes a preaching narrative is the point at which it is told with some biblical purpose in mind, to give some clear direction on the biblical message, to call people through the characterization to act in response to God's Word. The preaching element is necessary in order for a story to become a narrative.

Naturally, this call to action may come in any number of ways. The character who tells the story may urge the congregation to do as he or she did or to beware of acting as he or she did. The preacher may be an interviewer listening to the story of a biblical character, and that preacher may find it easy to bring the message to full light. The point of the narrative may be left up to the members of the congregation to sort out for themselves, to gain some insight into their own lives through the story which has just been told. But the biblical point must be made. The preaching narrative is storytelling with a purpose. It has a biblical focal point toward which it moves. And the narrative method moves its hearer toward that Word of God. William James said it well: "What holds attention tends to determine action."

As the preaching narrative is examined in the course of this study, the primary focus will be upon the pulpit use of the narrative. However, some of the most effective situations for the narrative may come at other times: youth retreats or conferences, Bible studies, service-club speeches, outdoor worship experiences, and special occasions (sunrise services, baccalaureate or graduation exercises, Maundy Thursday Communion worship, and Thanksgiving or Christmas Eve services, to name just a few).

In the chapters ahead, ideas for beginning a narrative will be considered (from different approaches to different types of narrative sermons from various preachers).

The steps in producing a narrative will be covered, including the necessary preparation before the actual writing begins. This preparation includes the study of background material.

Next, the purpose of the narrative must be clearly defined ahead of time. Then the passage of Scripture is chosen and exegeted, and the point of view is carefully selected. (The point of view determines who will tell the story.) The actual writing process comes next: characterization, inclusion of color and imagery to make the story come alive, use of details, figures of speech, and how to handle biblical weights and measures.

The next chapter will deal with rewriting, the use of costume and properties in the delivery of the narrative, and the art of assuming a character.

Finally, the delivery of the narrative is examined, including the most effective way of telling the story with emphasis on the beginning and ending of the narrative. The study concludes with several assorted preaching narratives, and in the final chapter there is a series of five narrative sermons used one Lenten season. An annotated bibliography is included, listing many books that are helpful in understanding the preaching narrative.

The preaching ministry of the church of Jesus Christ can surely be enhanced through the use of the narrative, and many people can come alive in their faith through this method of sharing the Good News and love of Christ Jesus. Such a study as this is offered with that prayer.

1 Places to Begin

The first narrative sermon I ever heard came from the lips of a campus chaplain speaking at a youth banquet. I was enthralled. Since then I have found the narrative to be one of the most exciting forms of preaching available to the homiletician today. I have used this style in many different situations.

Most often when I share a narrative on Sunday morning, I remain in the pulpit. Sometimes a change of preaching *method* along with a change of preaching *place* can lead to confusion among the congregation. (One summer morning, I remember, when I was filling the pulpit for a vacationing pastor, I stepped down into the center aisle to share my story of the rich young ruler—a story of wealth and position. One fellow told me later that he "tuned me out" because it was his impression that I was bragging about my situation in life.)

On special occasions in the Christian calendar I have found the narrative to be especially helpful in getting beyond the "expected." One Easter morning the shouted words "I won't believe it!" rang out, accompanied by the sound of palm slapped on the pulpit, and one man sat bolt upright, startled, and remained so during the rest of Thomas's story. He mentioned later that he was just beginning to settle down to hear the usual Easter fare, but because of the narrative, he gained a fresh understanding of the power of the resurrection.

About twice a summer our church took its worship service to a neighborhood park, and we would worship outdoors and spend the day together. It was always an excellent opportunity to present the gospel message through the eyes of a biblical character (a disciple of John the Baptist, a man crippled for thirty-eight years, or Simon

Magus, the magician). I found that narrative preaching held the attention of all members of the family no matter how young they were.

Admittedly, the narrative sermon is a far cry from the typical Sunday morning homily. But to members of any congregation the preaching narrative comes as a refreshing change of pace, style, and approach that results in a new interest in the importance and seriousness of the biblical message. I have found the narrative to be one of the most effective means of sharing the gospel of Jesus Christ and the message of the Bible.

As the narrative is studied, it must be noted that there are as many different methods of presenting such a sermon as there are preachers who do it. Frederick B. Speakman's usual manner of narrative is to begin with a third-person approach, an interviewer who confronts the biblical character. The biblical character then tells the story as Speakman moves from his interviewing role to assume the personality of the biblical character. See Speakman's *Love Is Something You Do* (listed in the Bibliography) for further examples.

J. W. G. Ward's typical methodology involves the preacher remaining the interrogator. Thus, the preacher may easily paint the scene and describe the character and story without doing so through the eyes of the biblical personality. Ward, then, *relates* the story that is told by the main character. (See the books by Ward listed in the Bibliography.)

Another preacher begins immediately by assuming the nature of the biblical person with no introduction. The story begins as the narrator tells it. On some occasions there are preachers who include other characters for which they involve members of the congregation. In those cases one story is told through the eyes of many people from many different points of view. Poetry may also be used so that the narrative is spoken entirely in poetic fashion. An example is "Priorities" in chapter 6.

Another possibility is to develop a narrative where several passages of Scripture are used to tell the story of one character. For example, the rich young ruler could move from his confrontation with Jesus to become the man of the parable who wanted to build bigger and better barns and end up as the rich man in the story of Lazarus and Dives.

The list could go on and on. The possibilities are unlimited. Generally, the idea of preaching the narrative is accomplished when the preacher puts himself or herself into the sandals of one of the biblical characters, or a nonbiblical character, and tells the story as that character would.

There is no guideline as to the best occasion for the use of the narrative since any time or any place is suitable to relate the message through the eyes of a biblical character. One may find ample opportunity to use the preaching narrative in any of the following ways.

The planned preaching schedule is an excellent beginning point. The narrative sermon can be used with any theme, and can enjoy any narrative passage of Scripture. (A narrative passage of Scripture is a pericope in which a short story takes place, where something happens, where there are people involved.) If the schedule calls for a sermon on the providence of God, a narrative on any of the lives of the patriarchs may be in order ("Abraham and Sarah Get a Son" or "Moses Leads"). If the plan includes a Sunday for preaching on commitment, the stories of the rich young ruler or Zacchaeus would be excellent choices.

Holidays and other special occasions are bursting with possibilities for narrative sermons. Christmas comes alive when Advent is celebrated through the eyes of people who surrounded the birth of Jesus (the shepherds, the innkeeper, Joseph, etc.). Lent becomes a moving experience when biblical characters share their stories (see chapter 7).

The possibilities are wide open for the preacher with an eye for character. As the Scriptures are studied, hundreds of stories leap off the pages as beautiful narrative passages, coming alive with personality and challenge.

The excitement is endless. Folks never get tired of a good story, and they find that the Scriptures are full of very human people, people with stories to relate about how God has moved in their lives.

Biblical characters become real human beings with whom twentieth-century people can identify (like the apostles or Amos or Mark). *Nonbiblical characters* can add insight to a story (a boy who keeps the stable where Jesus is born, or a cross-maker). *Historical figures* are able to speak in unique ways (a Puritan preacher on the second Thanksgiving or Constantine explaining his reasons for Christianizing the Roman Empire). The potential is endless. The benefits are overwhelming.

But where exactly does one begin? Ultimately, no matter what type of character is chosen, that character must be drawn or related to one passage of Scripture. The narrative must focus on one distinct passage of Scripture from which the story may begin, end, or complete itself. Whether presenting a character study in a pericope or a thematic study, the narrator must be grounded in some biblical happening, some event. That is the place to begin.

Once the situation for preaching is known and the purpose defined, then the Scripture becomes the most important part of the preaching narrative. And that, ultimately, is the most important place to start.

2 Background Material

One discovers a new depth to the story presented in the Scriptures through an ongoing study of biblical life. A sense of reality and wholeness grows out of an understanding of the details of life that are not usually mentioned in the text. For instance, sandals were always removed before entering either a house or a place of worship. Vinegar was sometimes used as a drink of punishment because of its acidic content. The shepherd literally lay down across the gate to the sheepfold at night to act as a "door." *Gethsemane* means "olive press" or "oil press."

Gathering background material for the narrative is one of the most exciting parts of getting hold of a good story. If any supporting details are manufactured by the preacher, then the story is falsified (if not for the hearers, at least in the mind of the narrator). An intensive study of the cultural milieu alone can bring a story alive with exciting points of interest. Countless narrative possibilities are generated just from research into biblical times.

There are many excellent tools available for such research, most of which may be found in the preacher's study, in the church library, or in the local city or township library. These are beginning suggestions for resource works.

1. *Bible dictionaries.* There is ample information in every Bible dictionary or encyclopedia (the multivolume sets usually contain more detail). All possible topic headings need to be researched in order to gather enough material. If the subject is "clouds," for instance, article headings such as "Weather," "Farming," or "Climate" will also need to be read.

2. *Bible handbooks.* There are many on the market, and some of them offer helpful information on particular texts or on some

region of the country, or they may provide up-to-date archaeological discoveries.

3. *Commentaries.* Many are especially helpful in giving background information on customs and biblical life (William Barclay's *Daily Study Bible Series* is very good for New Testament background).

4. A *Bible atlas* is an excellent tool for clues as to positions of various territories, layout of geography, and distances between towns.

5. Any good *church library* will be loaded with books on all types of background information, including artwork, volumes of photography on the Holy Land, and biblical novels.

6. Specific reference material may be found in the *local library.* Encyclopedias can be extremely helpful for background study. The index volume of each set is the best place to begin any search.

7. There is much *other material* that contains references to biblical background, including sermons, other narratives, periodical articles, and all of the books listed in the Bibliography of this book.

8. Introductory *textbooks* in biblical studies contain much information regarding history, culture, and other aspects of the biblical story.

9. There are a number of *texts* specifically related to general biblical background, as well as other specialized books on mythology, archaeology, history, and almost all other fields of interest.

These are mere starting places for gathering background materials. As the actual writing of the narrative is begun, there will be details to fill in and other more specific research to carry out. Those types of details are best handled after the writing has begun.

However, the most effective use of background study will be carried out before the narrative is written. If an idea has been generated by a passage of Scripture, then all possible historical, cultural, socioeconomic, and religious research ought to be carried on. It is important to understand as many aspects of the biblical world as is possible. Following are many helpful areas in which to begin the study and areas to research as the narrative writing progresses.

1. *Weather and climate.* Are there four seasons in this part of the world? Does the wind blow? How? From which direction? Do storms arise suddenly, or do they take a long time brewing? What kinds of storms can be expected? Do the people dress a certain way because of the weather? Would weather be a conversation "filler"

for people in biblical times? How did the people think the gods contributed to the weather during this particular time?

2. *Habits and customs.* Following are some areas that will have an effect on any biblical character:

a) *Worship.* How did the people worship? What procedure was followed? Where did different types of people sit in worship? How did they sit? What did they say? How did other religions affect synagogue worship or Christian worship of the time?

b) *Preparation of food.* What type of food was eaten? How was it prepared? Was most of it cooked, or was it eaten raw? How was it cooked? Where did it come from (was it imported)? How much would it have cost?

c) *Water.* Was it plentiful? Where did they have to get it? Could it be stored? What was water-gathering time like? Who got it? How was it carried? What was it used for?

d) *Eating habits.* How did they sit when eating? Were utensils used? What kinds of foods were eaten? Was there a particular order of eating? Did everyone in the family eat together?

e) *Clothing.* What did these people wear at this time of year, at this period of time? Were headdresses used? Did the women usually wear a veil? What was worn on the feet? How about underclothing? Was there specific clothing for cold weather?

f) *Farming.* What kinds of practices were followed? What kinds of animals were used? What was farmed? How was it planted? How was it reaped?

g) *Culture.* What art forms were practiced? Was dancing a common activity? How about singing? What types of musical instruments were used?

h) *Education.* How did a student learn? How old were students? Who did the teaching? Where? How much education was needed before a person could be called "learned"?

i) *Thinking.* How was thinking accomplished? Was logic in widespread use? Did biblical people understand the world differently from the way we do? Was there any type of scientific understanding?

j) *Medicine and health care.* What types of medical care were available? Who were the doctors? What kinds of treatments were offered? Was medication given? Were there hospitals? How was death handled?

3. *Archaeology.* Scientists, specifically archaeologists, are discovering many things year by year, and archaeological finds greatly

influence the details of any narrative. For instance, an area of the Tower of Antonia was excavated in 1870 that revealed large blocks of stone, which some scholars identify as the Pavement of John (19:13). Archaeology has been helpful with the location and description of the Pool of Beth-zatha of John 5. Of course, some narrative details will only be guesses, but they will be educated guesses once research has been done.

4. *Geography*. What was the terrain like? Is this village on top of a hill or in a valley? How does a person get from this town to the next? This question must be asked if the character moves from one city to another. The scene will be painted in more realistic terms if the narrator knows what is happening in terms of direction, distance, and the kind of territory through which he or she passes.

5. *Occupations*. If this character has an occupation, it is good to find out as much about it as possible. What sort of work did it entail? How much was he or she paid? Did this occupation require any special training or education, or could anybody do it? Was a special skill required? Was it handed down only within a family?

6. *Social structure*. What kinds of racial and sexual barriers were there? How were members of other races treated? How about class structure? What happened to sick people? What was the status of women? How were children taken care of?

7. *City and rural life*. If the narrative character comes from a particular city, what was that city like? What did it export? What were its cultural strong points? What were the houses like? Shops? Where were the farms located? What was it like to live on a farm? Where were the animals kept?

8. *Government*. What was the government like at this time? How was this particular region governed? Were the officials lenient or oppressive? Who was in charge? Was he or she strong? How were orders carried out? If the territory was occupied by foreign troops, how extensively?

9. *Flora and fauna*. What kinds of trees and shrubs could be found? What were they like? How tall did they grow? How full? What sort of animal life was found (domestic and wild)? Were there any vicious animals? What types of birds? How about fish?

10. *Time*. How was time kept? How was the calendar year divided? How was the day understood? Was the pace of life slow or fast?

11. *Money*. How was it earned? Were there banks? What procedure was used for spending money? What was used as money—coins, stones, or goods? What are equivalencies in today's terms?

12. *Weights and measures*. How much did various things weigh? How often were weights and measures used? What are equivalencies?

These are mere suggestions for beginning a study of background material in biblical and historical times. Details that are discovered through such research will greatly enhance the story since people will remember small details like the color of a man's robe, the length of a woman's hair, or the kinds of vegetables that were grown in a garden. More specific material will usually come to light as preparation continues for a particular narrative.

However, there are three things to remember as background material is pursued, especially in light of a particular narrative.

1. Not all of the background material studied will be used in the narrative. It will be very helpful for the preacher's preparation in gaining an understanding of the times in which the character lived. But some of this interesting research may surface only in a word or hasty reference. The purpose of background material is not to show off a well-prepared script. It is simply to give the preacher an adequate understanding of the times with which he or she is dealing. All of the research will not be used in the narrative, as the story then would be carried to illogical lengths. The study of the biblical milieu will help the preacher aid the congregation in visualizing the scene as the character moves through it, will bring a sense of authenticity to the story, and will certainly help the preacher understand many things that he or she may not have realized about this particular Scripture in the past.

2. Not all of the above areas of research will be employed for every narrative. In fact, only one or two of these areas may actually be used in any way each time. The benefit of the study will come in a broadened general knowledge and will be useful for later reference work and in general preaching.

3. The narrative should include only specific details and items. Otherwise there will be confusion. For instance, agricultural pests were many: cankerworms, caterpillars, ants, and locusts (to name a few). When the narrative is written, it is best to stick to one item rather than to list them all. "The locusts swarmed that year," is much easier to handle than, "There were ants and cankerworms and caterpillars and locusts that destroyed our wheat." Such a list will confuse the listener (especially if several lists are used in each narrative). It is not wise to attempt to impress a congregation with a great number of facts. Such details must always be governed by the purpose of the narrative rather than clutter it up.

Once background material has been uncovered, then the passage of Scripture must be exegeted. It will be necessary to understand the purpose of the pericope that is being used. The Greek or Hebrew texts may be helpful for possible shades of word meanings. The translation of certain phrases and proper names and terms may be very helpful in determining what happens in the story or in interpreting the meaning of an incident. As with any exegesis, various English translations of the Scripture will be useful since a particular version may offer a key understanding of the passage.

This type of background work is extremely important in determining legitimate material to fill in any narrative, to help bring the story alive for the people, to help involve them in its telling, and to bring them forcefully and compellingly to the purpose of the message.

However, one does not have to be an expert in these areas in order to use them. The above suggestions are simply focal points of things to look for as the preacher prepares the preaching narrative.

3 Selecting and Writing the Narrative

Having examined beginning points and adequate background materials, the next step in the process of preaching the narrative is that of focusing, condensing, and putting together the narrative. This perhaps is the most important phase in the process of the preaching narrative. There are three areas that will be considered in this chapter: (1) defining the purpose of the narrative; (2) deciding on the point of view; and (3) preparing the narrative (the actual writing of the tale).

The Purpose

The written purpose of the narrative will define the emphasis and direction of the story—even more so than the biblical material itself. The theme or purpose of the work will guide the speaker in determining the subject material and the background to be explored. (Some interesting background material may not fit the purpose of the narrative; so the purpose is written before the process of writing is begun.) The purpose should be specifically stated at the beginning of the writing procedure, and all events and paragraphs and incidents that happen in the telling of the story, or all of the commentary by the narrator, ought to be in relation to the main theme. The entire story must point toward one purpose.

Again, the preaching narrative is more than just an interesting story. It is a sermon. And as in any sermon, the narrative calls people to action on some point of the biblical message. That is, the narrative must work to change the behavior of the hearers, to change their opinions or attitudes, or to offer them some valid Christian truth. As William Thompson writes: "The point of the sermon is that this information will result in some change in your way of life."[1] That statement is important for the narrative. The point of the story or the purpose in its telling must be directed toward the end result of producing changed behavior. If each narrative works toward that end, remarkable results will follow, with people on all hands turning more directly to face the intended biblical message.

The first step in the writing procedure, then, is to define the purpose of this narrative. The next step is to choose the most appropriate Scripture (narrative passages are easier to handle). Perhaps the purpose has been set on some aspect of commitment. Good narrative passages are the stories of the rich young ruler (Mark 10:17-31) or Abraham and Isaac (Genesis 22:1-14). If the purpose is focused on stewardship, the parable of the rich man and his barns (Luke 12:13-21) is an excellent source, or a narrative using Paul's words in 1 Corinthians 16:1-4. If the topic is humility, the parable of the Pharisee and publican (Luke 18:9-14) could be used, or Moses standing on holy ground (Exodus 3:1-6).

Three general guidelines will be helpful:

1. Small passages of Scripture are easier to handle than larger ones. For instance, it is easier to deal specifically with a parable rather than the introductory material to it (one need not include Jesus' confrontation with the teacher of the Law while using the parable of the good Samaritan in Luke 10:25-37). In a larger story, such as Moses meeting Pharaoh, the text concerning the plagues would be easier to handle than the entire story of the Exodus. Where the narrative is based on one story that covers several chapters of Scripture, a few select verses may help to define the purpose.

2. For characters who are described more extensively in the Bible, it is much easier to take one incident for a narrative rather than a much longer span of time. Judas's betrayal in his relationship with Jesus is easier to deal with than his entire Passion Week activities. It is far easier to concentrate just on Mary Magdalene's reaction to Jesus' resurrection rather than have her tell her entire story. God speaking to Elijah on Mount Sinai is enough of a story to manage without including all of Elijah's life history.

3. There are always exceptions to this procedure, depending on the setting, the time alloted, and the purpose of the narrative. The entire span of an Old Testament war or feud could be handled very nicely through the eyes of a character. One story can be based

[1] William D. Thompson, *A Listener's Guide to Preaching* (Nashville: Abingdon Press, 1966), p. 44.

on two parables, as has already been described. Such an inter-weaving of the Scriptures can be a powerful presentation of the narrative style. Generally speaking, however, the shorter passage or the shorter story is easier to handle.

Point of View

Basically, then, a narrative sermon is a present-tense telling of a story. When the purpose of that story has been defined and the passage of Scripture selected, then comes the next step in the process of the preaching narrative. That is the choice of a point of view.

As in any writing, an established point of view is advantageous to the telling of the story. For instance, one point of view can allow the hearers to understand and see everything that is happening. In the same story another point of view can shield both the narrator and, thus, the congregation from finding out what is really happening until the very end.

There are five basic points of view which can be used in the narrative:

1. *First-person participant.* The narrator is the main character. He or she thinks and feels as the character would, expresses emotions as that character would and acts just as that character would act. "I" becomes the only storyteller in the narrative. This is probably the most commonly used point of view for the narrative. (See any of the narratives in chapters 6 or 7.)

2. *First-person observer.* The observer in this case may be a non-biblical character who watches and comments on biblical happenings. He or she simply observes what is going on and makes appropriate comments and assumes logical conclusions. The first-person observer never knows what the main character is thinking but can only draw inferences. (For an example of the first-person observer point of view, see Speakman's "What Pilate Said One Night.")

3. *Third-person omniscient.* This narrator knows everything that is happening. He or she can get into the minds of all the characters involved in the story, knows just what is going to happen (the story is perhaps being told at a later time), and the motivation is known for all participants. This type of narrative is more like a short story. "I" never gets involved in the story (or, at least, is not the main character). "He" and "she" are the more common pronouns. (For an example of the third-person omniscient point of view, see Speakman's "What the Passenger Told the Captain," in *Love Is Something You Do.)*

4. *Third-person limited.* The third-person narrator who is limited in scope can only follow the character, make comments, and let the scene move around him or her, much like the first-person observer. However, while the first-person observer is active in the narrative, the third-person limited is never included. The story, again, is told like a short story ("Then he did this," and "Then she did that."). The third-person choice of point of view is the most difficult to handle because it is harder to tell the story vividly as it is happening to someone else than it is to tell the story as it happens to oneself. The most effective use of third person comes when the observer gradually moves out of the picture and lets the main character speak personally. (For examples of third-person limited, see Speakman's "Requiem for a Treasurer" in *Love Is Something You Do,* in which an interviewer relates the story, or "One Soldier's Prayer," in which the narrator overhears the soldier's story.)

5. *Objective.* The objective narrator simply tells what is happening. He or she is outside of the happenings, again, and is simply relating what is going on. There is no judgment involved on the part of the narrator but only a hearing of events and dialogue. No commentary is offered, no remarks on the details, no personal involvement. The entire story is told in the third person. Since this point of view detracts from the purpose of the narrative, it should not be used, at least initially.

So Peter may tell his own story directly to the congregation. Or an interested second party may relate Peter's story on his behalf ("He told me that . . ."). Or a third person may overhear the story between two others. He or she acts as a reporter, adding his or her own commentary and letting the audience know everything that is happening in the story. Or an interviewer may seek out the main character and ask questions but add no thoughts of his or her own. (In the latter two cases the interviewer has no part in the story. He or she is completely outside of it.)

Several different points of view can be used in one narrative, as has already been mentioned. The narrative thus becomes much like a drama, with people involved, each telling his or her own side of the story or adding a segment of the events. Often members of the congregation are glad to fill in the other parts.

Suppose, then, that the story of the rich young ruler has been chosen. The point of view may be that of the rich young ruler himself, telling his story. Or the story may be approached through the eyes of one of the disciples (which would add another dimension to the event and may be useful for a different purpose). Or in order to observe all the actions of everyone, a passing camel driver may stop to see what is happening. Both of the latter two points of view are first-person observer.

As another alternative, the rich young ruler may be sought out after his confrontation with Jesus and interviewed for the congregation. The preacher/interviewer would add personal insights to the story as it progresses but would always keep the rich young ruler in the third person. (This is an example of third-person omniscient.) As still another possibility, the rich young ruler may just be interviewed without any additional comments on the part of the interviewer. The preacher would let the story speak for itself and would keep out of the action. This approach is called the third-person limited.

Each of these points of view brings a slightly different focus to the story, and each within itself is a separate narrative. A hundred variations could be offered. But a point of view should be chosen which most directly aids the purpose which has been written for the narrative.

Understanding the Narrator

Once the purpose has been written, the Scripture selected, and the point of view decided upon, the next step is to begin to visualize the narrative. Before doing the actual writing, it will be helpful to get a clear mental image of the character:

1. What does he or she look like? Are there any unusual characteristics that will add to the characterization? What would the character wear (both in biblical times and in these days)? Would this person dress like a bumblebee in a whirlwind or be as crisp and tidy as a snare drum? Rich or poor? Young or old?

2. What sorts of unusual character traits can be added that will aid in the development of this narrator? Is there a limp? Has he had leprosy? Are her sandals always too tight? Is he exceptionally vain? These types of "human" characteristics will make the story more believable and the preaching more effective.

3. How does this character react to strangers? What is some background material on this person? Could that background fit into the story? If a second or third individual comes into the tale, how will the main character react to the presence of another? (In Speakman's "Yes, I Remember Bethlehem" from *Love Is Something You Do,* the narrator makes the speaker comfortable in his own way—by offering tea in a dirty cup.)

65231

Tips on Writing

Once the character is firmly planted in the mind, then comes the actual writing of the narrative. The most important thing that must be kept in mind during the writing of the story is to be conscious of letting the hearers *live* the story.

As the narrator *lives* through what is happening, with emphasis on thoughts, smells, sounds, colors, and imagery, then the hearer will be involved in the same story. The narrator should refrain from preaching and should concentrate on *experience*. Exposition (filler material where there is no action) should be kept at a minimum.

In writing, experiencing a story will take much more time than merely telling about a story. This is illustrated in the following example: "It was a hot day when we went to Jericho" can better be rendered:

The burning sun seemed to be beating upon us, as it usually did when we picked our way along that lonely road down to Jericho. The dust was moving as the hot breath of wind flung it swirling around our exposed legs and only added to our uncomfortableness. Jericho seemed a long way away that day, but then, as we were coming over the last crest of hill, there she was, settled in a coolness that I couldn't wait to experience. As we descended on the city, I felt the heat of the sun melt away in the condensing coolness of the sycamores that lined the road.

Here is another example: "The thief hung on the cross and was in much pain" can better be experienced in the following manner:

The half-starved thief was panting for breath. The pull on his arms was tearing his chest muscles, and searing pain was ripping across his back. Already he could feel the skin flaps of his scourged back scrape against the rough wood of the cross.

And another: "The leper was shouting, 'Unclean,' because he was diseased" is better put:

His weak voice came forth, penetrating the scuffling crowd once again: "Unclean! Unclean!" Instinctively I moved away as he came poking through the milling shopping place. Even from ten paces I could see the white blotches of the disease eating away at his nose.

Details are perhaps the most important part of telling the story. That is why it is suggested that the scope of the narrative be confined to a small framework. In so doing, there is more room for detail to involve the congregation in the experience of the story.

As the narrative is written, it will be discovered that action verbs are most helpful, as well as words describing colors, noises, tastes, emotions, and other sensory stimuli. Use of the five senses will be extremely important in the experience of a story. Color and identifiable images help make the story come alive.

Speakman in "One Soldier's Prayer" writes:

> The young [Roman] soldier stood at the one large window of the room, bathing. He sponged off his body with the fresh water from the copper basin . . . and deliberately let its coolness pour down over his thirsty skin, turning now and then to stand erect in the window while the unseasonable breeze that had followed the thunderstorm played over his body.[2]

As the scene is painted and as the character or characters are introduced, opportunities will present themselves to recall some of the background material which has been studied. Some of it will come immediately to mind. Other material will have to be researched in the process of writing the narrative. (For instance, in the paragraph just quoted, *copper* was in ample use during biblical times. *Bronze,* an alloy made of copper and tin, was in common use, the first evidences of it being found before Abraham's time. However, *brass,* a copper-zinc alloy, was not invented until after biblical times. Including a brass basin in the story would have been careless, and that detail could be checked out almost immediately in a good Bible dictionary.)

As the writing progresses, figures of speech ought also to be kept in mind. Consider the use of similes ("He was as nervous as a fig leaf in a rainstorm"), metaphors ("That man was an angry crocodile"), and onomatopoeia ("He hit the ground with a hollow 'thud'"). Figures of speech ought to be kept in accordance with the defined character as well. It would be silly to have a bumbling caravan driver saying: "Jericho is a jeopardizer of saints." He would more likely say, "The city where we's goin', they don't pay no mind to preachers." As the writing is done, it is important for the speaker to stay in character.

In the writing process one other guideline is encouraged. Particular items should be singled out instead of broad ideas. (Rather than writing, "We could have had oxen or donkeys to plow with,"

---

[2]Frederick Speakman, *Love Is Something You Do* (Old Tappan, N.J.: Fleming H. Revell Company, 1959), p. 71.

just to show that both are used in plowing, it is wiser to limit the comment to a single thought: "Them oxen wasn't pulling good that day." The next time a narrative is written, the "donkeys" can be used.)

The fun of the narrative comes in the writing. The story develops itself as the writing progresses. Following the biblical story is important so that the audience will not be confused as to what is happening. However, it must be remembered that biblical conversation is not necessarily complete, and the narrative writer ought to feel free to fill in conversation that seems disjointed. Excessive exposition should be avoided. The story and the characters must breathe and come alive.

Weights, Measures, and Distances

The difficulty of dealing with weights and measures and distances is a perplexing problem in the writing of a narrative. Not many people today know how much a talent is worth or how long a cubit is. Units of weights and measures and money may easily be translated into miles or pounds or dollars. That can be done without sacrificing the biblical milieu. If that is not done, people will be caught in the trap of trying to figure out how much such and such is equal to and will lose the story line.

However, if specific weights and measures of today's terminology will distract the listener, those items can be alluded to in other ways: "The boat was as long as a city block!" or "It cost her a whole year's wage to buy that perfume." Such comparisons allow the listener to catch on quickly to size, cost, distance, and weight.

The difficulty in this area comes in knowing where to draw the line for each particular narrative. If there is a specifically biblical narrative, any reference to something contemporary (like a cola bottle or an abandoned tire) may be distracting. On the other hand, if the entire narrative is modernized (finding Mary Magdalene in the red-light district), then the contemporary references can be helpful, from counting dimes to fishing from rowboats. The writer, however, must be careful not to mix the setting.

Beginnings and Endings

Just before this chapter is concluded, there is yet one more area of discussion. That involves the beginning and the ending of the narrative. It is helpful to get the audience involved as soon as possible in the story. A scene may be painted, the story may open with a smashing line, or something dramatic may be planned so that the people get "on board" quickly. As the character, the narrator, reacts to things that happen, so the congregation, too, will react. Of course, different types of beginnings need to be tailored to the type of situation and people addressed.

As the ending is approached, the purpose must again be called to mind. If the purpose has been remembered throughout the telling of the story, the ending ought to be decisive in wrapping up the whole progress of the tale. Sometimes it is taken for granted that the people will have understood the message. That is not always so. People don't necessarily get the point of the narrative. It is easy for them to get caught up in the story itself, so that they may not be conscious of there being any purpose to its telling.

There are two ways to finish, then. The first is the "preachy" method, in which the character or narrator ties everything together and brings out the full meaning of the story, in which members of the congregation are moved to respond consciously with their lives or are challenged in some way.

The other possible ending is to leave the story with the listener, much as David Kossoff does in his *Book of Witnesses* (see Bibliography). The character tells his or her story and lets the audience draw its own conclusions. If the purpose has been adequately stressed in the process of the narration, this idea may be the most effective means of conclusion.

In the first narrative I wrote, the rich young ruler told his story. It ended with his walking away from the audience, saying, "That's a difficult thing to do—give up everything I own and my place of honor in the community. I can't make that kind of commitment of my whole life—not right now. It's just too hard. It's just too hard." The purpose in that ending was to get people to examine their own commitment to Christ. There was always someone who got the message, but most of the time the majority of the people thought it was a nice telling of a Bible story and weren't moved by any message. They could as easily have gone to the theater. I have found that this type of open-ended conclusion is not the best for driving home the point of the story.

There may seem to be an overwhelming amount of material to remember in writing a narrative. However, the main focus of attention falls in six areas that have been discussed:

1. The purpose is to be narrowly defined at the outset, and that purpose should be remembered throughout the entire writing process.

2. A shorter passage of Scripture is easier to deal with than a lengthy one.

3. The point of view is chosen that will best bring out the intended purpose of the narrative.

4. The character should be mentally noted and defined at first and then sketched in as the writing progresses, with quirks, speech patterns, odd movements, and other human characteristics.

5. Sensory images are the best writing tools for the narrative: color, sight, sounds, tastes, texture, smells, intuitions, emotions, and the like.

6. Exposition is to be kept to a minimum. The story should be experienced in the telling, as if it were happening right now.

These six steps are basic to preparing a vivid, meaningful, and challenging narrative, the kind that will most effectively present an exciting biblical message.

4 Preparation for the Narrative

As inconspicuously as possible during a hymn before the sermon, the preacher slips out the side door of the pulpit area. The hymn concludes, and the congregation is seated. And when all is quiet, the preacher reenters in costume, a long flowing robe with headpiece, and walking with a limp.

On another occasion the minister has been dressed in a black suit, white shirt, and skinny black tie. When the time comes for the sermon to be delivered, he dons a pair of wire-rimmed spectacles and assumes the character of an old man. He becomes Nicodemus.

Such are two dramatic beginnings for the narrative style. Each is unique. The first could not possibly be used in certain pulpits. In others it would become a definite help to set the stage for what is to come. The second method demands that the preacher assume the character without props or costume. It takes greater acting ability, but it can be used in any pulpit to help the congregation follow the story that is to come. This chapter will examine the preacher's preparation for the delivery of the narrative so that such delivery may enhance the story itself.

Rewriting

The first step in preparing oneself for a narrative is to rewrite the rough draft of the manuscript. After the first draft has been written and as that draft is studied, loose ends will be evident that need to be tied up. As the story is read through, it must be examined from the congregation's point of view. Will there be items they won't understand? Was the narrative begun on one theme and then suddenly changed to include another theme? Are there items that don't fit the purpose? Are there dangling pieces that will leave people wondering?

As the initial draft is written, the character may develop certain traits that weren't present at the outset. The character may have picked up a hearing problem which was not taken into consideration at the beginning. That will need to be written into the story. She may speak with a lisp later on. The lisp will have to be part of her speech through the entire narrative. Perhaps red hair will add to the effect of the conclusion, but that wasn't accounted for at the inception of the character.

In rewriting the narrative, six items should be noted:

1. Character traits must be examined (as mentioned previously) so that the character is consistent throughout the story.

2. The narrator's vocabulary or speech patterns must be carried through. Sometimes when a narrative is written in three or four sittings, the mood of the writer at each sitting will affect the development of the character. There may be changes in life-style from page to page. The character must be consistent throughout the story; so those types of changes have to be credible.

3. Sometimes an important element in the story may come to mind too late in the initial writing process. Such an item should have been included earlier in the story but was not thought of at the time. ("Oh, I forgot to tell you that it was getting dark" is more easily incorporated earlier in the story as "The night was falling.") As the first draft is being written, those "late-remembered" items ought to have been noted at the time so they will be at hand for the rewriting. Some of the material from the original manuscript will need to be rearranged. Other things will logically come in the order in which they were first written, but for dramatic reasons they could make a greater impact if they were inserted sooner or later in the story.

4. As the rough draft is scanned, the audience must be kept in mind. Every detail of the story must be remembered. Nothing should be assumed. For instance, in the excitement of telling the story of Abraham and Isaac, the servants accompanying the two to the mountain are mentioned. But then there is no further mention of them. They have been forgotten. The story must be told through the eyes of the one who was present through the event, and what that character sees, the congregation must see. An audience should never be left confused about any character or any situation in the story.

5. As much as the writer tries to keep away from exposition, there still will be much of it in the rough draft. Long paragraphs of exposition need to be spiced up. Are there figures of speech that

can be added? Can the material in this paragraph of exposition better be experienced than described? Is there enough color and other sensory images here to keep the story moving?

6. Finally, the story must flow in unity. There must be a beginning, a middle filled with movement, and an ending that is conclusive. The purpose should be foremost in the mind of the congregation. They need to know what they can do now, once the narrative is finished.

Rewriting is one of the most rewarding habits in the process of preparing a narrative. It is hard work, but the main direction and wording of the narrative have already been done, which is the most difficult part of the narrative work. Rewriting involves marking up the manuscript with a pen, rerouting some of it, tightening it up, adding some additional touches, and preparing an outstanding piece of work. Scissors and rubber cement are excellent rewriting tools, as well as different colored marking pens. Additional background material may be inserted along with fresh metaphors in place of worn-out clichés. Other character traits may make the narrator more human.

The narrative must then be typed in final form. It will still need to be edited in many ways as the writing is done, but the best narratives are free flowing and generous where the writer feels free to depart from the original manuscript. The rewriting itself should be done in one sitting so that the language and character gain strength of continuity.

Costume and Makeup

Once the writing is completed, it is then time to begin to consider the situation in which the narrative is to be presented. What will the setting be (outdoor retreat around a campfire, church sanctuary, school auditorium)? What is the particular situation (youth meeting, formal worship service, baccalaureate service)? As the setting and situation are examined and thought through carefully, the approach that the narrative will take should be altered as well as the extent of the use of costume or properties. The movement of the service must be considered as well as the order of worship and where the narrative will be delivered. Is there a chance to exit before the sermon? Will this narrative be given from the head table of a large banquet hall where donning a costume will be impossible?

The same narrative can easily be adjusted to any setting or situation (once with the use of a costume, the next time with only a prop). Once the particular milieu is determined, the next step is to make definite arrangements for the narrative. As the situation is evaluated in terms of the narrative, it must be decided just how involved the costuming should become in adding to the intent of the message without destroying the reverence of worship for some. Each situation will be different.

In unknown circumstances it is best to prepare with minimal costuming or props. A small amount of "helps" can be very effective in defining the character without having an overwhelming burden of clothing or makeup for which to be responsible.

In regard to costume, something as simple as a Christmas pageant robe will add delightful effects to the narrative. Almost any church will have a boxful of costumes. Sandals are usually good additions. It must be remembered that the costume will be determined by both the situation and the narrator. Careful research in the area of costuming is important.

If the narrative is strictly set in biblical times, the costume will necessarily be biblical (if allowable circumstances are at hand). If the character is contemporary, suitable current dress is appropriate. There may be times when a biblical character will fit into modern dress, which can be helpful in making a transition in the message of the narrative. (For instance, for my rich young ruler, I am accustomed to wearing a blue plaid tuxedo jacket. It is simple, yet sets the tone for the character. On another occasion, I used a modern carpenter's apron for a narrative of a cross-maker. I found that the apron was distractive because it had advertising for an electrical supply house on it. Some people wondered what was in its pockets. It is wise to choose costumes carefully.)

Makeup can be another important part of a narrative. Again, the situation will determine its use. However, the extent of the makeup will depend upon two things: the nearness of the audience and the light in the situation in which the narrative is given. Next to a campfire, for instance, there is no need for facial makeup (with the exception of a mustache or beard) since it could not be seen. Likewise, if the congregation is seated below and fifty feet from the pulpit, they will not see any detailed makeup. Naturally, certain situations will not allow time to use makeup, and it is better not to use it than to apply it hastily as an amateurish job.

There may be an occasion, though, when the opportunity will be available to use makeup. Wrinkles can be created by using a wet eyebrow pencil over the existing wrinkles in one's face. There are grooves in the forehead as well as beside the upper lip and cheek, under the nose, under the lower lip, not to mention dimples on the chin and cheeks. The wrinkles need to be overemphasized, especially with intensive light. A scar can be added with facial putty available at any costume or magic shop. Dark makeup can be used effectively to create shadows in low areas of the face (the hollows of the eyes and cheeks and under the chin). Lighter makeup, or highlighting makeup, will create high cheekbones, an extending brow, or a broken nose. Makeup, if properly and creatively applied, can greatly enhance the characterization which is being presented to the congregation.

There may come situations in which a mustache or beard would be appropriate. A cheap costume wig or beard may be used, but generally they look false and will only add to an unprofessional presentation. It must be remembered that the costume is used solely to bring out the character who is to speak and, more importantly, the message. If a beard is used, it must be fastened down securely. The narrative ought to be practiced with the beard in place to assure ease of movement. If the beard needs adjustment, strands of wig hair combed out and glued or stapled to cheesecloth will add many creative additions to a beard or hairpiece. These sideburns or mustaches or goatees may be stapled together. However, again, any facial hair that is used must be able to withstand movement, especially of the mouth. Any costume and makeup shop will carry useful items for the narrative preacher. There are some very fine coloring sticks suitable for changing the appearance of hair. They look like large tubes of lipstick, come in all colors, and can lighten or darken eyebrows, mustaches, or fringe hair around a head covering. They can also enhance the effect of aging when that is the desired impression.

The most helpful tool I have found is a package of double-stick makeup tapes, about one inch in width and three and one-half inches in length. They are excellent for gluing on facial hair, stay put even under bright lights, and come off in no time. Except for the tape pieces, there is no easy way to glue hair to the face. Spirit gum, the professional hair glue, works very nicely, but it is not easy to remove quickly. Adhesive tape or other glue may work on a cool morning, but on a hot day or under hot lights perspiration loosens tape in short order. (Once when I used adhesive tape for facial hair, one of my eyebrows slipped off right at the climax of an old shepherd's story. Wanting to keep my face symmetrical, I inconspicuously removed the other eyebrow, and while only a few people noticed, they made sure I remembered it.)

Props

There will be many situations in which it is impossible to wear a costume or use makeup. On those occasions it may be helpful to use a prop that can identify the narrator. Such a prop may be either a small piece of costume (a tuxedo jacket, a cap, or a carpenter's apron). Other props may be some object that adds to the characterization (a candle carried on a saucer, a large book, a walking stick, an umbrella, a glass of water, or a sword). As the narrator of the story is pictured in the mind or as he or she has been developed in the unfolding of the story, what type of prop would especially fit? What would give the audience a quick understanding of the character? What single item would identify this person?

Thus, costume, makeup, and props can be useful in the development of a narrative. The purpose of each is simply to enhance the character and so to aid in the projection of the message.

Assuming a Character

By far the most interesting type of interpretation that can be done is to *assume* the character rather than use costume or makeup or props to identify the person. In assuming a character, the preacher must have the personality fully understood so that actions, movements, patterns of speech, use of the voice, and facial expression are all identifiably those of the narrator.

One good method to use when assuming the character is to take several hours observing a person in life who most resembles the envisioned character. If that narrator is an old man, the preacher should spend time observing an old man, making careful notes about dress, walk, speech, and physical movements. Of particular interest should be the use of hands and feet. They are two of the most potent convincers of character. The preacher, in assuming a character, will have to *become* that character.

When assuming a character, the narrator must, at the time of delivery, let the type of character so fill him or her that nothing of the preacher is remembered by the congregation. That type of character-becoming is the most rewarding for both the narrator and the listener.

Titles

There is one last topic that needs to be discussed in relation to preparation for the narrative. Where there is a printed program, a title will greatly add to the effect of a narrative. I had been in the habit of simply titling any narrative sermon "A Visit" in hopes that my congregation would be able to identify that title with the coming of a narrative. However, that was not always the case. (Once I was preaching about irrational fears and called the sermon "Phobias." One member of the congregation was psychologically prepared to hear a narrative about a young man by that name.) In the course of using "A Visit," I abandoned some excellent titles that could have been used.

When a title is used, it is important that it draw the audience into the story. Speakman and Ward have some very helpful titles ("What the Shopkeeper Told the Strangers," "Requiem for a Treasurer," and "The Salty Tang" are examples). Clever titles are just as important to the presentation of the narrative as they are for any other sermon.

And so, with adequate preparation, the time comes to deliver the message. It has been wrapped up in one beautiful narrative package, and now comes the great unveiling—the presentation.

5 Delivery of the Narrative

Unmercifully your heart is pounding its way out of your chest, your palms are sweaty, and your greatest concern is how this is going to come off and how you will look to your people. With your legs feeling like water, you step into your pulpit and begin your story, stumbling here and there, halting, perhaps losing your predetermined place, but sensing the growing story and characterization that are such a very great part of your spirit. And, you find, when your last words are spoken, that there has been a new kind of attentiveness through it all and an exhilaration, and even months later your people are still talking about that "sermon."

All of your hard work at writing the narrative has now come to its most important emphasis, that of the actual delivery. Sermons are written to be preached, not read, and your purpose in writing your narrative has been for its telling. The past weeks' tribulation has its outpouring in the preaching of your work. The time has come. The congregation waits with startled ears to hear what the Word of God is for the day.

It is important that the Scripture related to the narrative be read at some point in the service if possible. There are times when such a reading is impossible. However, people today seem to be so out of tune with the Bible that frequently they aren't sure what is an allegory and what was an actual happening. (Once, after presenting the rich young ruler at an outdoor concert, a girl thanked me for the nice rendition of that "parable.") One must be careful, though, not to make such a reading of the Scripture redundant. That is, if the narrative passage is read, immediately followed by a narrative presentation of the same material, it can become very boring. It is wise either to read the passage earlier in the worship experience or to insert enough background material at the beginning of the story so that the biblical setting is clear.

The stage is set. The program has led up to the sermon. The hearers are eager. The preacher assumes the planned role from the outset or leads the congregation to another character who tells the story.

Beginning in Character

While any kind of introduction may be suitable for your narrative sermon, it is not always necessary to introduce yourself. Sometimes one of the most distracting beginnings for a narrative is to announce: "This morning we are going to learn about the story of Abraham and Isaac, and I am going to tell the story through the eyes of one of their servants. His name is Pedro." Such a beginning takes the speaker out of his or her assumed characterization and moves the listener away from the extraordinary and unique style that the narrative brings with it. (Keith Miller begins his "Inside I Trembled" in this manner. I found the introduction to be a distraction to the rest of his excellent presentation.)

The most effective introduction of a narration is to begin in character, whether the character is an interviewer moving through a scene to meet the actual storyteller or the character begins with his or her story directly. If the opening sentence or the props or the costume are effective, people will get the idea quickly as to what is about to take place. They are intelligent people. They have come looking for something to challenge their life-styles, and they will include themselves in the story as it progresses. Words of introduction are not needed to force people into the story. Sometimes the speaker will be halfway through the narrative before some of them figure out what is going on, but that startling revelation adds to the punch of the narrative style.

Sharing the Story

A narrative is an eyewitness account of a biblical happening (with the exception of historical or contemporary narratives). As such, it is most effective when told, not when read. There is a certain freshness in a story that is presented as if for the first time, as it is happening, as it is remembered, as the scenes are pictured in the eye of the speaker's mind. The experience becomes a shared one between the narrator and the congregation.

The best kind of narrative delivery, then, is one offered without manuscript, without notes, and, most effectively, without memorization. When the speaker steps into the pulpit, the character should be firmly fastened in mind so that the speaker knows the manner of walking and gestures and patterns of speech. Because this speaking situation is different from the environment in which the narrative was written, the characterization may not be just the same as the written one. That is fine, but the character must remain consistent throughout the story. I have also discovered that, from one presentation of a narrative to another, the character will change slightly. That always has added a freshness to the story and its message.

Once the characterization is fixed in mind, the speaker should know the *general* movement of the story (which is to be expected, because the speaker has written it). The *direction* may be memorized, but it is not necessary to memorize the words or metaphors or sounds. Memorized storytelling is as impotent as one that is read. Instead, the scenes should unfold before the narrator as he or she moves through the telling. If there is a clear mental picture of the course of events in the narrative, alive with vivid color and sensory images and crisp conversation and certain actions and details, then the narrative will flow smoothly as if it were just remembered for this occasion, for this audience.

Two things are to be kept in mind. First, there will be some details that will be forgotten but will be remembered later on. In the process of telling (not writing), the speaker will have to decide whether that forgotten detail is important for the story or not. If so, it can be inserted at any point. That happens when anyone is telling a story. It keeps the narrative alive.

Secondly, it is helpful to remember that the congregation or listeners don't know the story as it has been laid out with all of the vivid colors and figures of speech. They have not read the manuscript. Consequently, they will never know when an image is forgotten or when the speaker misspoke. The congregation will not recognize a forgotten detail inserted at a later time. To them, it is the first time this story has ever been told. And the process of telling it makes it a genuine eyewitness account with natural human factors inherent in the process of remembering. Such a real presentation will help to bring the people face-to-face with the intent, the purpose, the message that comes from the Word of God.

The most effective sort of narration occurs when the preacher pictures the scenes as they unfold and shares them with the audience as the character moves through the story. A lot of details do not have to be remembered. All of the research and writing and rewriting will add to the telling as the preparation comes to mind. Details come naturally if the homework has been done. If the speaker has labored to include smells and sounds and sights and colors in the writing, then those images will come through in the telling. There is no shame for forgotten detail because of the progression of the narrative. The listeners will have experienced the story.

If the narrative is approached in this way, it will naturally change in its telling from occasion to occasion. That keeps the story alive. Details that were once forgotten can then be reincluded in the next telling.

Beginnings and Endings

It is important that the story should begin at one point, at a well-defined place or point of time. This will help orient the audience. The story should carry through in its telling, in the experience, moving logically from scene to scene, remembrance to remembrance, and conclude at the end (or at the finish of this particular incident of Scripture). The purpose must be held at the forefront of the speaker's mind as it has been outlined. At the conclusion of the telling of the story that purpose should be reevaluated in light of what has been said in order that the strongest case possible be made for getting the point across. Has the story progressed toward its intended purpose? Has it been clear enough so that it need not be restated? If not, how can the story be summed up in its conclusion to bring home the message?

The beginning points and ending points may vary from situation to situation, from telling to telling. For example: If the main character has a limp and the limp is mentioned somewhere in the narrative to prove a point or illustrate a truth, then the limp becomes an important part of the story. However, should the speaker wish to present the same narrative from a banquet table, with no room to demonstrate the limp, such a reference will be impotent. As the narrative is considered, it may be wise to change the handicap to a dead arm, or a lisp, or a stiff neck. Whenever such a change is made, it must be carried throughout the entire narrative so that there will be the necessary continuity to provide an effective message.

It is helpful, also, to keep the beginning and ending flexible according to each setting so that the story may begin with a reference to the local situation. Smooth transitions are a bonus for an alert speaker. Thus from a few introductory remarks about the immediate circumstances (especially if he or she is a guest speaker) the narrator can then lead directly into his or her personal story. (Once, when asked to say a few words about our church's history in a neighboring pulpit, I moved directly into the narrative with the words "Well, that's some background on our church. Now let me give you some of my personal background.")

In concluding the narrative, the same principle holds true. It may be natural, according to certain traditions, to add a distinctive, evangelistic conclusion and an "altar call" to a narrative. However, in another situation using the same narrative, the "altar call" would be out of the question, and the narrative could easily end, "Well, that's how I met Jesus, and I wanted you to know about it so that you may consider knowing him, too."

The sharing of the narrative is one of the most exhilarating experiences there can be. Certainly it is the climax of the entire writing process. As the story grows, the speaker has the fixed attention of the congregation. As the character lives through the preacher, as the scenes are painted, as the congregation is involved in the story, and as the emotion of the narrator is shared along with distinctive expression and mannerisms, then the Good News is being preached and brought home to its listeners. And that is the goal of the preaching narrative.

6 Assorted Narratives

Included in this chapter are six narratives that have been used on various occasions.

The first, "Man by the Pool," was delivered at an outdoor worship service in a neighborhood park. It was an informal setting, with people sitting on the ground, in lawn chairs, or at picnic tables.

The second, "Annas," was given in the church sanctuary on Maundy Thursday evening. It was followed by a Communion service.

"What Raphael Heard" was used at a Christmas Eve service, with a candle-lighting ceremony afterwards.

The fourth narrative, "Zacchaeus," was first used around a campfire for a youth camp. It was adapted for a Sunday morning pulpit.

"A Puritan Thanksgiving" was preached at a community Thanksgiving Eve service in a school cafeteria. It is an example of a historical narrative.

Finally, "Priorities" is an example of a poetic narrative, used in a regular Sunday morning worship experience.

Man by the Pool

Scripture: *John 5:1-18*
Purpose: *Commitment to Jesus involves responsibility for our lives*
Prop: *A rolled-up mat carried under the arm*

I guess I should be grateful. After all, I *was* a poor, lonely, broken-up cripple for thirty-eight years. Thirty-eight years. I can remember back then when this unfortunate accident happened and all hope was gone for life. There was no more reason to live. A broken body is useless. I had to learn to accept my lot in life, though bitterly, and had to drown my pride in sorrow because I had to learn to depend on others. The spirit-filled world around me had no compassion—even the gods take no pity on a cripple. I've never known what it's like to have a good friend. I had to be dependent on people. I had to use them to take care of me, and there weren't many who could stand me after a week or two.

I had heard of Beth-zatha, just outside Jerusalem. Beth-zatha, Pool of Angels, with its curative powers. And one day when the demon in the trees and the demon in the skies and the demon in the earth all rebelled against me, a pitiful cripple—when the heavens opened and drenched me with heavy, hot drops of rain, and the wind blew fiercely, kicking the prestorm dust into me and through me (hair, eyes, ears filled, nostrils caked)—I knew that I couldn't stand life one more day without the aid of Beth-zatha. I knew of a friend, a sheepherder, who was going to Jerusalem that week, and he dragged me on a little cart down the bumpy, jerking, perilous road to the Holy City, town of hope, and citadel of the healing powers of Beth-zatha.

We entered the city through the northeast gate—the Sheep Gate, as it was named in the vernacular—the gate through which sheep were to enter the temple area for sacrifice. Beth-zatha itself was outside the city walls: two pools next to each other, down four staircases, with five columns there. My friend (now sick of my orders and irresponsibility, for which I cannot help myself), carried me down near the water's edge and fled my presence. The glimmer of hope I had known was now a reality, but the place didn't seem to me to be very special. I knew, though, that the spirit which infested this pool had strange and great powers of healing. I dragged myself to poolside, inserted my foot into the pool's cooling water, and heard some bit of snickering behind me.

I turned. A wretched old beggar was crouched against the wall, grinning toothlessly, slapping the pavement. "You dirty the water, cripple," he said. I angered. I grew furious. How dare he, one who is able to walk, poke fun at a poor crippled man who could not care for himself. I spat. He flinched.

"The angel of this pool does not heal until he stirs the water. You will see."

"I have come this far," I answered, "to sit at the edge of this pool and cool my feet and seek healing from Beth-zatha, and you tell me, O scum of the earth, that I must wait for him to stir the waters? You are beneath dignity." I spat at him again. I dragged myself into the cool shade, waiting, listening for bits of information that would be helpful.

I discovered in the weeks and years to come that the pool would occasionally bubble and its surface would be disturbed. It was then that the angel of mercy was visiting the pool, and the first one into the pool was the one who would receive healing.

Each time I clawed the dirt, straining to pull myself into the cool recesses of the pool Beth-zatha, to be healed by this angel, and each time I was the last one in the area to reach the pool. There were mobs of us who would stay at poolside day in and day out. Sometimes a stranger passing by would descend to the waters, nearly fainting from the heat above, and would plunge his head under the healing waters as the pool bubbled up. He would go on his way rejoicing. A stranger stealing our healing powers—the healing that belonged to us who were residents! Some at the pool would beg for scraps of food that we would share. Most went along their way after a few weeks of waiting, claiming that the pool's disturbance was an underground spring and the legends were mere superstition. I'm glad they went their way. They spoiled the fellowship.

I became a figurehead of the pool of Beth-zatha. I could tell stories. I would be the one to curse at strangers and drive them away. I had been there now for twenty-two years, the longest of any resident. Others would feed me, take care of me, but always someone new. They called me a crotchety old man.

And then that day a new man, a strange man, came slowly down the steps opposite my corner of the pool area. He walked with determination, looking at all of us seated around the pool, nodding and speaking to some as he reached the bottom step. As he walked around, rubbing shoulders with all of us invalids, appearing to be friendly, I saw someone sitting off in a corner raise his arm and point an accusing finger at me. The stranger nodded and came toward me with a brisk walk. He had his eye on me all the way. I hardly had time to put on my "watch out, I'm mad" face. But as I watched him move through the crowd, I could see that something was different about this man. I could tell that he wasn't even interested in our pool of water.

He came over, stood looking down on me; others turned about and stared at this stranger who had come into our midst and apparently were surprised that I had made no moves yet to drive this foreigner away. As this man stood there watching me, my heart began to beat faster and faster. My breath became short. I licked my lips. He said to me, "Do you want to get well?"

My first thought jumped to the healing waters of the pool of Beth-zatha. "Oh, but sir," I said, "I don't have friends here to put me in the pool when the water is stirred up. There's always someone else, someone younger, someone quicker, or some stranger, who gets to the pool before I do." I thought perhaps he'd take the hint and get lost. But he stayed right there, staring at me, as if I were some sort of special creature.

"Do I want to get well?" I asked myself. "Yes!" "No!" I am secure here. I have friends. I have food. I have companionship. My meager needs are met. But look at this stranger—one who has the audacity to ask me if I want to get well—so full of life, with such strong limbs and a certain heartiness. Yes, I'd like to be well. I'd like to be strong. Then I'd have it made.

The stranger spoke again, disturbing my thoughts. All he said was, "Get up! Pick up your mat and walk."

I wanted to argue. I hated what he said, and, more than that, I hated whatever he was trying to do to me—make an obvious fool out of me in front of my friends. I wanted to reach up and scratch that man's face. But no words would come. No movement. He had some sort of authority, and he was *commanding* me to get up and walk. I hadn't walked for thirty-eight years. But I felt a strange, surging, exciting power. My legs and arms began to shake, and there was strength. I got on one knee, one foot up, the other while both hands were on the ground, still shaking, wobbly, I could stand on my legs, steadying myself against the wall. The shaking subsided. I took a deep breath and a step. The pavement under my feet was an entirely different sensation than I had remembered. It was something new, something precious, pavement under my feet as I walked. I was healed! I was healed.

"O God," I cried, "O God of Israel! I am grateful." And I walked to my mat, picked it up, pushed it under my arm, and walked, slowly, up the steps that led out to the sunlight, and the busy crowds, and the bleating of the sheep, who were just entering through the Sheep Gate for the feast.

I walked on the dusty roads, I ran, I tripped and fell. What a sensation! I picked up my mat again and headed for the temple. I took three steps and stopped dead in my tracks.

I was healed. I knew strength. I was excitedly joyful. But I suddenly thought, *Now what?* Now, instead of being dependent on others, of being the center of attention, of never knowing any responsibility, now I was going to have to work. Now I was responsible for my own life. Suddenly, after thirty-eight years, I would have to take some responsibility. And I knew just then as I walked toward the temple, that that man, that stranger with the power of God in his veins, had played a dirty trick on me.

I was wondering what I ought to do as I strolled into the temple area, where I was going to go, what sort of job I could get, when one of the rabbis came up to me and shook me. "This is the sabbath," he bellowed, "and it's against our Law for you to carry your mat."

I looked down at the mat under my arm. I didn't want trouble with the religious leaders after my healing. "But the man who healed me told me to pick up my mat and walk." I turned away from that guy. I had more important things on my mind. His Law didn't heal me. Nor did the magic waters of Beth-zatha. That man healed me, and I knew he must have been from God; so I was going to the temple to thank God or to argue with Him about this nasty thing He'd pulled on me.

That busybody rabbi yelled after me, "Who was the man who told you to pick up your mat and walk?"

I stopped. I hadn't thought to ask the man's name. I just didn't know. I hadn't thought to find out who he was, or what his name was, or what he was dong there at Beth-zatha. And that lack of knowledge, compounded with the fact that he had played a trick on me and all of the other thoughts in my mind, caused me to turn around and shout, "Well, I just don't know the man's name. I just don't know who he is."

I walked over and sat down, grumbling. What am I going to do now? I haven't done a thing since I was a boy, had people waiting on me, feeding me, carrying me. I could shout orders and get response. Now I was on my own. I had to get out and find a job. I had to work and take responsibility. Now if I barked orders, nobody would be apt to listen. I'm strong now. I can do things myself. That stranger's touch brought responsibility, and I don't like it. I sat pondering, two to three hours, about what I was going to do *now*—now that I wasn't a cripple. Then I looked up and saw him again in the temple, and he was coming over to me. Now what did he want? Hadn't he already ruined my life? What was he going to expect of me? How much was I going to have to pay?

He marched up. "Look," he shouted, "you are well now. Quit your sins, or something worse may happen to you."

Quit my sins? Sins? And it dawned on me. My grumbling. My bitter attitude. My resentment. My unwillingness to accept responsibility. Sins. I guess he was saying that if I didn't accept the responsibility he'd dumped in my lap, then I'd be worse off than before. He had turned his back and walked off. I got up and went over to another man standing there. "Who is that man?" I asked. "Which one? Oh, that's Jesus, the Galilean. Some say he is the Son of God and call him 'Master.'"

"The Son of God? He healed me," I said. "He made me whole. He set me free from the useless hope of Beth-zatha. He set me free from my physical binding. He just now set me free from myself and my self-centeredness. The Master touched me and made me whole. With the Master's touch comes responsibility, and I'm not sure what that responsibility means. But I'm going to follow him to discover that responsibility, and I'm going to work at my life. He made me whole, and with that wholeness comes work to be done."

I turned away from that man and ran into a group of rabbis. "That man was Jesus, Jesus the Galilean. He's the Son of God, and he healed me," I shouted. And I went on my way to find Jesus and follow him.

I guess I should be grateful. And each day I guess I am more and more grateful.

Maybe you'd like the Master to touch you. And with that touch will come responsibility. No longer will you be allowed to do everything for yourself. You'll have to accept the responsibility that comes with the touch. You'll have to follow him and work and know that you are his now. And I'll tell you, the responsibility that comes when Jesus touches you is not an easy thing to handle. Take it from me. You've got to work at it. Some of you have been touched by Jesus, so you say, but you haven't bothered with the responsibility. You've got to quit your sins. You've got to work at the responsibility that is before you. And you've got to follow him.

He's given me new life and a new hope and new freedom. I may not know much, but I do know that the Master touched me, and I have decided to follow him.

Annas

Scripture: *John 18:12-14, 19-24*

Purpose: *Jesus disturbs those who will not believe*
Costume and Prop: *Robe, slippers, patchwork nightcap, carrying candle*

What time can it be anyway? Dawn must be about to break. Here I am, the great Annas, and I've let one man, one lousy rabble-rouser, upset me more than anyone ever has. I must be getting old, losing touch. Somehow, I don't feel the same. Well, a night without sleep is one thing, but a night filled with the likes of that man. . . . My temper gets away from me.

Ah, Annas, Annas, easy old boy. Think back. Were you not appointed high priest by Quirinius? Did you not hold the powerful office for eight years? But when you were thrown out by that dog Valerius Gratus, you, in all of your wisdom, managed to hang on to the power of that office. Ishmael was thrown out, and your son, Eleazar, took the throne while you remained in command. And then Simon, another inept scoundrel, and now Joseph Caiaphas, husband of your daughter, brought the power back into the family. And don't you keep tight controls on Caiaphas? Ah, yes, Annas, you hold the key to all of Jerusalem in your pocket.

So why should one rebellious teacher upset you so much? Oh, but what he's done, upsetting my trade, probably ruined the business for all time, and the bazaars of Annas will fall quietly by the wayside, going bankrupt, and my silver-lined pockets and castles will crumble into dust. And all because of that one man.

I've had to work for my money, slaved with my hands (hardly respectable for one of any fame), invested heartily with what I could pilfer from the less fortunate. It took money to get my position, a slight collaboration with the Romans, a little wining and dining for those who count, a little money slipped under the tunic to buy a vote to get me the power I needed. And once in office I had the perfect plan to get all the wealth I needed. It was brilliant and has brought me fame and prestige and more power than any other man in Jerusalem.

Being high priest, it is my job to see that the commoners' sacrifices are fit for the Lord. I've set up inspectors in the Court of Gentiles. It is their job to examine the sacrifices brought from outside the temple. The Lord demands the best, you know, and sacrifices must be without spot or blemish. My inspectors examine the sacrifices, usually to find a spot or blemish (a pair of doves can be purchased for about twenty-five cents outside the city)—those are cheap birds. The pilgrim has no choice but to buy one of our animals for sacrifice (a pair of doves runs about two dollars here) which have been previously inspected. Don't get me wrong; we are allowed, according to the Law, to make a small charge for this service. The pilgrims who have come to the city at Passover time have grown in number to such an extent that one day's earnings at the bazaars can net enough to live on comfortably for a year.

And then four days ago the whole system was disrupted. That insane Galilean, Jesus from Nazareth, came riding pompously into Jerusalem, in semblance of a king, and made a fool out of himself. He came back the next day and cleaned me out. Grabbed a whip and scattered my sacrificial animals. Overturned the tables of my merchants, coins flying every which way. A little slave boy came running to my chamber that day, shouting that the Galilean had made a mess in the temple, and I rushed there to see what further blasphemy he had pronounced.

The temple court was a shambles. Most of the coins had been stolen by dirty scum of the city, groveling in the dust; but the money that my people had managed to get back was hardly enough to pay for a janitor to clean up the mess. I went directly to Caiaphas.

I cannot say how pleased I was when I discovered that already plans were being made to kill this hypocritical bumbler. The priests of the Law had decided to do away with the man before the feast so that the people wouldn't be incited to riot. We were all conscious of ways to get him—not merely to put him away, but to get him out of our way—to kill him. The best plan would be to hand him over to the Romans and let them deal with him—crucifixion isn't bad enough for that Jesus.

Yesterday one of his followers— Judas—played right into our hands. A greedy scoundrel, he wanted to give Jesus to us, at night, for money. We counted out thirty pieces of silver. With a grin he told us he would make arrangements, and he fled. I demanded at that time that I would see the teacher first. No one dared go against my wish. And I, with my powerful influence, spoke to the Romans about crucifying this man. Pilate himself said that we'd need a charge against the government.

It was some time in the middle of the evening that Judas came to us last night. "If you want him," he said, "this is your last chance. I will lead you to him." We summoned the temple guards, and I sent a runner to Pilate asking for soldiers—to tell him that we were going after a criminal against the kingdom of Rome and might need some help. The soldiers met the guards at the temple and went out to the Mount of Olives to get Jesus, with instructions to bring him here first. I had no desire to go with them to arrest this man. Someone in my position doesn't do the dirty work. He sends someone else to do it for him.

Soon I heard the clatter of a crowd, and I knew that they were bringing the man to me. I could have him for as long as I pleased, and I was going to make him sweat it out. His life or death rested in my hands, and I wanted him to come groveling before me on his hands and knees, begging me to let him go free.

And there he was, flung into the room, bound in chains. He stumbled. If we had been outdoors, I would have kicked the dust in his face. The soldiers and guards must have been silent on their way back from the Mount. They all filed into the great hall, and, seeing me staring at my competitor on the floor, they all began to talk at once. They were shouting some nonsense about falling on their faces before this man, and something about Malchus getting his ear hacked off and healed by Jesus. I raised my hand and silenced them. I did not want that ruckus here. I wanted to face Jesus with a crowd to attend to him should he get out of hand or try some of that magic on me. Jesus had struggled to his feet by this time.

"So," I said, "you are Jesus, the Galilean. What do you want with me, fool? I want you to know that I can have you crucified (arrangements have already been made), or I can let you go on the promise that you'll never come near me again or this city."

I waited to watch him weigh my words and sweat a little. He remained calm, staring at me, saying nothing.

"What do you want of me?" I shouted. "You've destroyed my business; you come riding into my city disguised as a king; you teach heresy. Who are you, anyway, that you think you can get away with that?"

He remained silent. I grew furious.

"How many followers do you have?" Silence.

"You have insulted the teachers of the Law, the Pharisees, by calling them hypocrites. Is that true?"

"You have heard so." It was all he said.

"Oh, so you do have a tongue. What sorts of things have you been teaching lately, Jesus, mighty Jesus of Nazareth?"

I had to get some word of truth out of him. I had to get him to say some blasphemous words so that I could condemn him.

He spoke again. "I have always spoken publicly to everyone. I have taught in the synagogues and in the temple, where all the Jews come together. I have never said anything in secret. So why do you question me? Question the people who heard me. Ask them what I taught. They know what I said."

This man was arguing with me, throwing the Law back in my face. No man can be condemned by his own witness, and Jesus was holding up that Law to me. I would have kicked him. One of the guards there slapped the man, turned him around. "How dare you talk to the high priest that way!" I would have done the same had I been close to Jesus.

Jesus responded, "If I've said something wrong, tell everyone here what it is. But if I am right in what I said, why do you hit me?"

I could get nowhere with the man. I was boiling and couldn't think straight.

"Get him out of here!" I screamed. "Take him away. Kill him! Do with him what you want, but I want to see him dead. If he wishes to throw the Law in my face, let the Law deal with him. Let the Sanhedrin meet at dawn, and I will be there, and we will condemn him to death. Take him away!"

They took him to the house of Caiaphas where they've kept him. Perhaps they could get some word of blasphemy out of him. It is almost dawn now. I must go. The Sanhedrin meets, and we must get him to Pilate to be crucified before the day is out. I want to see him dead, hanging, suffering on a cross. Then we'll see what God thinks about this man who would be high priest, who wishes to provide a sacrificial system for common folks to get righteous. We'll see. We'll make him a sacrifice all right! We'll get him crucified! If you're smart, you won't be following him either. If you just listen to him, he disrupts your life. If you follow him, you will die in the process.

What Raphael Heard

Scripture: *Luke 2:1-20*
Purpose: *Jesus' birth brings many joys*
Costume: *Robe and sandals*

It has been a silent world for Raphael. That's me, Raphael, but I'm happy now. You see, I was born deaf, deaf as a dead star. But that never held me back. My mother used to push me to get out on my own, get a job, do something worthwhile. Oh, I looked for work but never could find any, what with my lack of education and the fact that I couldn't hear. Then the Goldsteins offered me work. We attend the synagogue together, and they knew I was looking; and my mother being ill and all, they gave me a job.

The Goldsteins, you know, have converted their upper chamber on the roof into a guest room for travelers. They wanted
Raphael to carry water and meals up there and to clean up the
stable. They are fortunate, not to have Raphael work for them,
but to have the stable, the cave under the cliffside from their house,
where they keep their own animals and the animals of the visitors.

Well, you, you who are here in Bethlehem also for the census,
know that our town is busy, busy, busy. Goldstein is a shrewd
man, you know (please do not report this to the authorities), and
he raised his prices. He got word that the census was coming, and
he raised his prices, knowing that we'd be busy. And he's had a
houseful for days now. And Raphael has been scampering up those
side steps a hundred thousand times a day, carrying dinners and
water and fetching animals for those whose business was finished,
and cleaning the stable every day. Our capacity is a comfortable
six in the guest room, but Goldstein has twelve in there and has
Raphael doing all the hard work and no bonus to show for it either.

Well now, let me tell you what happened today. Late this
afternoon, just before dinner, this couple came into town. She was
awfully pregnant, any dumbbell could see that, and was only about
twelve or thirteen. He was twice her age—a working man. His
hands were scarred and beaten and rough (I have learned to see
things like that since I could not hear). This poor couple wanted
a place to stay, and Goldstein pointed up to the guest room several
times shaking his head, and grew somewhat impatient with them
as they pressed him. The man gestured at his wife's pregnancy and
then, with a shrug of his shoulders, Goldstein had an idea. Now
Goldstein is a shrewd man, and I saw him point down toward the
cave under the cliff where the animals were kept, and he disappeared
into his house and came out with a fresh torch and lit it for them,
and gave it to the man; and then Goldstein had his hand out and
the man dropped three coins in his palm and off they went, slowly,
down to the cave, pulling an old donkey behind.

I wanted to rush down there to clean the place up a bit before
they got there, but Goldstein knocked me on the ear and pulled
me inside and handed me the tin plates with dinner for the guests
upstairs. I made six trips up there, and then, as was my habit, he
sent me home before I cleaned the stables.

Now I wanted to go to the cave before I got my own dinner,
but Goldstein hadn't given me anything to take down to the couple;
so I thought I'd go home and get my dinner and bring what little
we could spare back to the couple, along with a clean blanket, and

so I rushed home and ate hurriedly and put a couple of sandwiches together and grabbed the blanket off my pallet, and rushed out into the cool night, with the briefest peck of a kiss for my poor ill mother.

And that is when it happened. As I was making my way back to Goldstein's, on the outskirts of the town walls—my own little shortcut—gradually, and almost imperceptibly, a noise began to break in upon me. My ears began to open, and the sound came rushing in on me like the sound that thunder must make when it shakes the earth. And it was dark and frightened me to death, so that I fell against the wall and rammed my fists up to my ears. And as I released the pressure, along with that confused, indistinct noise carried in from some far-off place, out from the hills where the sheep lay at night there was such sweet music, of a thousand faint voices, coming gently carried in by the breezes. It seemed heavenly and so faint that I thought I was dreaming. And I thought at first it was the sound that sheep must make, but I know differently now.

And when that roar gradually subsided, and the sweet singing, I began to hear other sounds, of something clomping behind me, on the other side of the wall, and I hoisted myself up and saw one lame man in the street, going home from business, and he turned a corner. And then I heard the wind which I had always felt so gently brushing against my cheek.

And, out loud, so that the sound of my own voice startled me, I shouted, "Raphael hears!" and I climbed down and had to decide what to do. I had sandwiches and a blanket and should go on to tell Goldstein, but I wanted so much to tell Mother, but, no, I was already almost at Goldstein's, but Goldstein wouldn't care, and finally, with tears welling up in my eyes from such a wealth of sound, I decided to go on to the cave and do my chores and not let on about my hearing and go back home after that.

And so I rushed on toward the stable, conscious now of all sorts of strange noises, but knew I couldn't stop to investigate. And when I arrived, I heard strange sounds—a struggling girl seeming as if about to die—and the man was standing outside the cave and clutched my arm and wouldn't let me go in and I heard some rustling and groaning and the man started talking to me and told me how they were having a baby, and that this wasn't any ordinary baby, but it was God's and I didn't know what he was talking about; so I handed him my blanket and the two sandwiches and said, "I'm sorry. I didn't bring anything for the baby." And he looked puzzled and started to say something, and said, "The blanket. You brought the blanket." And I said, "Yes, Raphael brought a blanket for the baby." And I was pleased. And then came a little squeal—then a cry—very loud. And the man took the blanket and the sandwiches and disappeared into the cave, and the man came back out as if to tell me something but rushed back in and hit his leg against the stone manger on the left (I've done that myself), and all I could see in the flickering torchlight was a huddled woman in the corner, using a rag to wipe such a tiny little baby; and the man took the blanket to her and the sandwiches and knelt down and touched the crying baby under the chin and came running back out and pushed me inside, and the mother wrapped the baby in some strips of cloth from the stable and then in my blanket and the man took the baby and put it in the manger and it went to sleep.

Now, I have been in that stable many times, but had never heard such sounds before. When the echoing cry stopped, the wind was there, swishing around the stone walls, and made the straw rustle. Our two oxen, Amos and Micah, were off in the corner snorting. There were donkey sounds, hollow hooves on the rock, and Eli the sheep was breathing heavily and there was some cooing from up in the dark above us. It sounded like a little family of doves—and I thought there were only two of them.

And the wonder of all the sounds overwhelmed me, and then I noticed that the man had gone back outside and was pacing, and the girl was huddled over in the corner, and I got my little rake and started cleaning. It suddenly dawned on me that a stable was no place for a baby.

I worked hard to clean up the place, being as quiet as I could, but then there was some noise outside and the man was speaking with some others, who were breathlessly telling a story, and I could hear every word about heavenly voices who told them about a baby born in a stable who was Christ, the Lord, and then they were singing, hundreds of them, and I looked out into the dark night, and there were several shabby men and a couple of boys younger than I, carrying shepherd crooks, and they had come to visit the baby.

And I knew that the voices they heard singing in the sky were the same voices that I heard when my ears opened. And the oldest man of the shepherds repeated the story, telling the man that the angels had told them that this was a Savior, and he was God's Savior, the Messiah. And the man nodded, and signaled for them to keep quiet, and motioned for them to come in and he lifted the blanket from the baby's face and they saw the baby squirming and the mother came over and sat next to the manger, and the shepherds kneeled down in the wet straw, and I stopped raking and knelt down in the wet straw and started to cry.

And the shepherds stayed for quite a while and then got up and went outside and the man went with them and then they went back home, to the hills. And I went about my work, listening to the strange sounds all around me, and, just as I was carrying out the muck, the baby started to whimper and then cry and the little mother reached over and picked it up and held it tight and started to sing a little lullaby, and I listened, and then I went home to tell my mother all the Good News.

Zacchaeus

Scripture: Luke 19:1-10
Purpose: Jesus is a friend and calls us to a changed life
Prop: A money pouch

Oh, what is the use—this, this monetary existence? A mere existence. There is no life, no purpose to life, no interest in life. All is vanity—yes, all is emptiness. And my heart feels just like this mansion I live in—ample, made of stone, plenty of room—too much room—and empty. All I can hear is the echo of my footsteps in the hallways, cracking off the walls. And when I work at my money, an occasional coin tinkles on the cold marble; and that tinkle carries through every room, sometimes crashing in my ears. Yet the emptiness isn't quite as bad as the loneliness—that dread, diseased loneliness. Oh, to hear the laughter of friends echoing in my plush rooms! To rejoice at the footsteps of little children. To sing with birds in my fountain-flowing gardens—but there are no birds. It is as if they, too, have nothing to do with me.

Sometimes I wonder whether it has all been worth it—or why I got into this racket in the first place, this dirty business, this work of swine, where the only friends one has are thieves. Oh, I know why I got into it all right, but has it been worth it? Well, you can see for yourselves that I am small of stature. While I was growing up, they used to give me the works—"How come you're always standing in a hole?—I think you forgot to put your feet on this morning!—What happened, did your father pound you on top of your head again?" And those were my friends! They called me Weasel and Short Stuff and Alexander the Little. No wonder I hated them all, and I took every measure I could to cut their throats. You don't know what it's like to have everyone looking down on you all your life. I am a Jew, and my friends were all Jews (if you could call them friends), and it took me a long while to decide how I could best get back at them—we would all be of business age at the same time, but I would collect their taxes for them, and there wasn't anything they could do about it, and I ripped them off royally. The best way, I found, to avenge hatred is to get to a man's purse. Within a year, I was alone, by myself—threats on my life and no friends. I had to let my wife go because she was getting in the way of my business practices.

And my attitude only got me better and better positions with the Roman government—they are the ones I work for. I have worked my way up from a tax farmer—collecting in a district—to chief collector, where many others pay me for the privilege of collecting taxes for me. And I think of that Levi-Matthew from Capernaum, who gave it all up a year or so ago. Little remuneration and, yet, he has friends. And what better place to settle than beautiful Jericho—Jericho, the winter capital of the kingdom, a land popular for its figs and tourism? And what better place could I locate than here, where taxes must be collected regularly (and heavily, I might add)?

I have acquired the most beautiful mansion in all of Jericho—in all of the world, no doubt. There are numerous servants who bow at my feet at the smack of my hands. There are gardeners who keep up my gardens and fountains, who trim the vines back along the many paths, who see to it that my gardens are the most beautiful in the land. But what a pity—people are so repelled at the sight of me that they will not come near. And I would pay a thousand talents if someone would be my friend, if someone would laugh with me and walk with me in my gardens. Money is treachery if there is loneliness.

I spend too much time sitting in my house, counting money, creating records, sending bills. And needless to say, I am no physical specimen. I try to get exercise regularly. So I go outside for a breath of air in the crisp morning, to jog a bit in the garden, to step outside my gates and watch for someone I can tax. And the air feels good, indeed, filling stagnant lungs with new life. Yet what is the real pleasure without friends? Look, all the people walk on the other side of the street—they will not bid me even a good morning.

But, are they not rushing elsewhere? Where are they going? What is this crowd gathering—this happy, joyous crowd? Oh, I must go there. Suppose I could rush up and throw my arms around someone and laugh with him and we could share this joy together? But they will not let me near—you will see. I hear bits of what they are shouting: "The Nazarene," "That carpenter, Jesus," "The One who is the Teacher is coming."

The Nazarene, Jesus? Coming here? You don't suppose that he would be my friend? Oh, if Levi, then why not me? At least, it would be worth a look—and if he doesn't become my friend in truth, he will be my friend of imagination! Then I will surely have a friend—and a good one at that! Oh, I must see. I must get through there—but there are only shoulders high above me and voices so that I cannot hear. Let me through here! Ooof—an elbow in the ribs! Do you hear that? "It's Zacchaeus—go on home, dog!" "Go back to your castle, sinner—the Teacher doesn't want to see you!" Ahhh! Was that a stick on the side of the face? It smarts.

They will not let me through here, but I am determined to see this Jesus, my friend. I shall go down the road a ways. A trip? And I am sprawling on my face. I get up, slowly, whisking off the dust, ignoring the laughter of children.

Oh, how can I get through? A glance up gives me the answer— that tree over there, a sycamore fig, with its low branches—I can hop up there, hide in its branches where no one can see me, and I can see this Master. Yes, that is what I will do. With one leap, I am on the bottom branch, and in two steps, I am hidden in the topmost part of the foliage—a good view, a good view, indeed!

There, down the road a way, you can see where the crowd is parting, the Teacher coming through. No doubt about which one he is, though he is not dressed extraordinarily. He is of average height, but with a certain air, a confident step, discussing with those nearest him, smiling occasionally from side to side, stopping to listen to someone, walking again, coming closer here, still teaching, the crowd closest to him listening to get some word of hope. And me? Oh, if I could but get some word of hope from him! The group following him is growing as he comes along, the crowd getting larger and quieter as they listen to him. He really is quite a young fellow to have such a following; I had expected him to be a bit older. He is strong and ruddy, smiling as he comes. Yet, somewhat gentle, but with confidence. I can see him approaching under the tree. He has a peaceful voice, soft, and, well, I just wish I could hear everything he has to say.

I almost fall, grab quickly, hang on, then fix my gaze on him again. The dust rises where they are coming, and slowly spreads itself in the crowd of tunics. The Teacher's voice rises slightly above the whispering below me.

And here he is! And he stops! Stops talking. Stops walking. He stops right under my tree. Oh, I hope he doesn't see me—call attention to me in this tree—the ridicule would be overbearing. All the people beneath become deathly still. And I have the feeling that I am in for it, that if he sees me, he is really going to point an accusing finger at me for being such a dog. Some of the men are beginning to whisper, and I am relieved. But before they can say too much, the Teacher is looking up—does he see me? Am I well hidden? But he fixes his eyes right on me.

"Zacchaeus, come down. I'm going to your house today!"

My house? And how did he know my name? He wants me to come down? Coming to my house? A great smile, and a good deal of nervousness. He wants to come to my house? And how did he know my name? I step down, onto the next branch—in my haste, twigs crackle, I scrape my arm, and come down another, getting more excited, and down, and, with a leap, I land somehow right side up in front of this Jesus. And I feel a little foolish, me, Zacchaeus, standing in front of the Nazarene, and excited, hopeful. Had he called me by name, and coming to my house? I am not able to explain it easily. And I am not aware of the pressing crowds at all, until someone breaks the spell by turning to leave: "The Teacher is going to the house of a sinner!"

And there is other grumbling that starts, others murmuring in consent, and shiftless men turning, but Jesus doesn't seem to be interested in what they think—I like this fellow—he really *is* my friend. But as he looks, my whole desperate life passes before my eyes, my hopelessness, my shame, my sinful ways, and I know that all I care about right now is that Jesus is standing here facing me and I am looking, gazing into his kind face, and the crowd is turning against him because he is my friend. In a moment, I know that I have been all wrong, that I am no good to myself, or to anybody else, or to Jesus, or to God. I realize that my monetary existence, stealing from these people their hard-earned money, is absolutely the wrong way to go in life, and that my whole thing is off course. I begin to weep, can feel the tears well up in my eyes, and I turn from him to break the spell.

I take a breath, knowing what I must do to have life, and I turn again to face him, and, in a moment of conviction: "Please, listen, Sir! I'll give half of all that I own to the poor, and if I've cheated anyone, I'll repay him, ah, four times as much!" That is far beyond what the Law requires, but I mean it. I know that I must follow this good Jesus.

Now, for the first time since I had come down from the tree, Jesus looks away—looks, turns to my accusers, to *his* accusers—and says with no embarrassment, "Salvation has come to this man's house today. He, too, is a descendent of Abraham. The Son of Man came to seek and to save the lost."

Yes, I am a lost child of Abraham—ah, *was* a lost child. In a twinkling, I have realized that now I am found again, because this Jesus, this Son of Man (do not some call him Son of God?) loves me—me, chief tax collector—me, social outcast, hated member of the human race—me, friendless and lonely. Now I have a friend!

I guess those in the crowd had to think about what this Jesus had just done. It is deathly still, and I, with an air of confidence, turn and, beckoning to Jesus and his close followers, signal them to follow me to my house—my empty hallways that now will echo with the laughter of friends! Oh, what a glorious day! What beauty does this life hold! What joy! And for the first time today, and in my life, I can hear birds singing, I can hear the gentle breeze rustle leaves, I can hear children playing together! I turn to make sure that Jesus is still following and his disciples—this is too good to be a dream. Me—Zacchaeus—with such friends as these!

Stealing and cheating and lying and living for myself alone are no more for me. This man has given me a new lease on life. *He* is my Lord, now, and no one else, and nothing else. Salvation as a gift just like that—handed freely—coming in my deciding to follow Jesus. It's a better way—making *him* Master. Instead of hating people, now I can love them. You want to see a changed man? Here's one—look at me. This Jesus really has something to offer.

You, too, may feel a need of him—to give you a new lease on life. He waits outside the door to your heart—to change you so that you can follow him and love others. Maybe you think you are not worthy. *I* was not worthy. Maybe you think he cannot change you. *I* was beyond help. But he did something to me, just from a look of confidence—a challenge to follow him. That's what I needed. You are wrong if you say that you do not need him.

A Puritan Thanksgiving

Scripture: 1 Thessalonians 5:16-18
Purpose: Be thankful in spite of hardship
Costume: Black suit, white shirt, black tie

The topic of my sermon for this evening, November 28, 1623, is as follows: *In spite of all our hardships, still the Lord provides for our needs.* I have chosen the preceding text because it aptly fits our situation. I have chosen this topic because I have heard no small bit of grumbling from you these days, and we must prepare ourselves for the celebration tomorrow. I wish to take this opportunity to refresh your memories which have seemed to be missing. Can you not remember how we, chilled and huddling, were crowded into that tiny ship, *Mayflower,* at sea for sixty-five long days and waiting for over a month with land in sight while scouts picked a suitable acreage for us? Perhaps you would rather be back in England? Have you forgotten that we left to seek a new place to worship freely? Mid-September, 1620, we got on board. And there stood Captain Christopher Jones and Sam Fuller, ship's doctor (who has since departed from us), and the five-man crew, and all the rest of us—103 in all (if *I* remember right), eating salted beef and vegetables and bread smeared stingily with butter. Can you not remember the joy of touching ground once again and beginning our first house on December 25 of that year? Have you forgotten how God brought us across the sea?

Oh, I will be the first one to complain of that first winter. Almost half of our colony passed away then—they, having found their promised land, were snatched away from there in the Lord's wisdom. But do you remember the first warm rays of the spring sun, the trickles of melted snow, and our friend Squanto who crossed racial barriers (a gift from God) to help us plant corn and teach us how to fish? Can you remember how we had to post watch at night that first spring to keep wolves from eating our fish fertilizer? And through it all, God provided for our every need, and He led us in His will. Indeed, sometimes we went a little hungry. Sometimes it was a little too cold. Sometimes we miss our loved ones who made the treacherous journey and did not make it through the winter. But we must consider *our* lives, how God has spared *us,* and how he has helped *us* grow during these past two years.

Look back those two years to our first great celebration of God's bounty, late in 1621, as I remember. For three straight days we worshiped. Some of you may remember my sermon at that time, entitled "Through the Sea He Led Us." And we feasted and we played together—a great celebration proclaimed by our own Governor William Bradford. Can you remember how four of you men spent the previous few days fowling and came back with enough geese, ducks, and quail to feed the entire colony for a week? And wasn't it two others who hunted all through that summer for deer so that we'd have more than enough venison? Was that not the hand of God providing for our every need?

And the Indians, the natives of the land, they did not *have* to be friendly. Yet they have helped us so wonderfully—surely you must see that that is another of God's provisions. We were saddened to hear of the epidemic six years ago that nearly killed them all, but perhaps it has been because of their small number that they are friendly. Was that not an evidence of Providence? It was only right to invite them to our first feast. They are so kind to us. But did we imagine that ninety of them would be joining us in our meal of thanks? And Chief Massasoit among them, being quite an honor in itself. And do you remember the rich venison they brought and the wild turkeys? Oh, a happy occasion that was—the corn bread and nuts and succotash—I, sharing my trencher with a young Indian lad. (You would think he had never eaten from such a plate before.) After having given thanks to the great God, Provider of all our needs, and having stuffed ourselves with these good foods and drinks, we left our tables and gathered for some games and athletics for the remainder of the afternoon. That was two years ago.

Yes, there have been some hard times since then. Unnecessary pilfering (a most unworthy occupation) among our own company, some youngster being whipped publicly almost every week. And last year that culprit (whose name I shall not mention) kept stealing from our Indian friends and, in spite of repeated warnings, continued to do so, much to the discomfort of the Indians. Because of the strained relations that were brought about, we had to hang the chap, if only to keep the natives content. The hard times continued—that day when the ship came in (which we initially thought was such a great provision from God's hand) with no other than Captain Christopher Jones at the helm, but we were only to discover that the prices were so high that we did not wish to trade for those necessities. I believe we disappointed them when we told them that we had gone for so long now without those things that we could go a bit longer because of the outrageous prices.

Yet the hand of God has provided in other ways. Through these difficult times God has a way out. Do you remember when there was a great famine in Canaan, and Israel sent his sons to Egypt to purchase corn, and Joseph greeted them there, and they were well provided for? We have no Egypt here to which we can go—no foreign land—but the sea is our Egypt—we are fed by the sea that is at our front door. God always provides a way.

And still you complain? Look back a few months—the third week of May, when the first breath of drought came upon us. Our corn was withering, even when packed with fish as Squanto taught us. We grew tired gathering nuts and berries and hunting for scarce waterfowl and shellfish. The fishing boats would stay out for five or six days, because to return empty-handed would only have brought more discouragement. It seemed even then that we had forgotten all about how God had led us through. He has been our Provider, and we had to set aside a *special day* of prayer and humiliation—mid-July that was, after two months of famine. You will remember that it was bright with the sun shining all day, and that evening the first clouds gathered, and the first drops of rain fell. Since that day we have had seasonable weather with periods of rain, and we have had a fruitful and abundant harvest, for which mercy we have set aside as a day of thanksgiving tomorrow, November 29, 1623—our second in the colony. You have already been gathering waterfowl and wild turkeys and venison to be put on great spits for the children to turn over the fires. You have brought in schools of fish and eels and shellfish. What a glorious day it will be tomorrow! A day of thanksgiving to God for bringing us through safely once again! How can you grumble so? Have you forgotten how God has provided? Through all of our hardship let us not forget how God provides. You may think that you have it pretty bad, but there are others who have come through it before, always with God leading. It is written in the Scriptures, "in every thing give thanks." In all of your difficulties can you so easily forget how God blesses you?

Priorities

Scripture: *Luke 10:38-42*
Purpose: *A Christian's priority is to learn from Jesus*
No costume

Hurry, scurry, hustle, bustle,
In my little kitchen room,
Wrestling with tins and ladles
And chowder all my own.
Is it not too much for one woman alone?

And there they crouch, Sister and the Good Sir,
Like a fat sow at her trough and her Master in the mud—
Sitting, molling over choppy wording,

Considering questions of the universe.
And what of me?

> Get the dinner ready, Martha,
> Serve yourself silly,
> While I sit patiently,
> And am entertained by the Good Sir.

Oh, is it not my duty to serve—
Is it not, I mean, *our* duty to serve
(Little sister Mary and I)—
As good hostesses of this Good Sir?
Should not *service* be our priority?

I am angered in the symphonic orchestration
Of my clanking pots and pans—
All to myself, alone am I,
And where is my sister-help?

> Get the dinner ready, Martha,
> Serve yourself silly,
> While I sit patiently,
> And am entertained by the Good Sir.

Oh, the pantry is full enough.
> What shall we choose, dear sister,
> For this Good Sir?
> This dented can of string beans?
> This half-rotted rutabaga?
> This moldy crust of dry bread?
Nay, there must be something better,
In behind all of this pauper's wealth.
There must be our very best for this Good Sir.
> And what of our usual dinnerware?
> (The stirring crackle of clacking tin)
> Eating can be such a noisy affair.
> But is that suitable for this Good Sir?

Nay, he deserves the very best,
Having come from afar—
And on his way to Jerusalem
(Where a thrashing throng will greet him, they say).
Not just *any* guest, he,
But a guest extraordinaire,
With such alhambrian air.

Oh, they have called him somewhat distant,
Not down-to-earth, but far-fetchy,
With his personable God-talk,
His message the same:
Give *God* your first priority.

And here he crouches now,
Distracting this sister mine from her appointed task,
Keeping her from doing her heaven-rewardable thing—
Service to this Good Sir is her priority,

But what does she?
Sits as a fat sow at her trough,
Slurping the good garbage of this Good Sir.
Can she not discover for herself
The priority of the Good Sir?

Oh, it *is* purely a matter of priority.
Does this Master need one more vagabond
To sit at his feet, anxiously awaiting
The nectar of righteousness wafting from his lips?
Cannot this poor dear Sir have a moment's rest
From his itinerant weariness?
Must he constantly be "Rabbi,"
And never "rested guest"?

   Oh, Mary, Mary—
   So confused at your priority,
   And with so much to be done in service
   To this kind Sir.
   And my two hands are scarce enough . . .

   (The tintinnabulation of clattering pans
   And crashing pottery—)

Oh, must it be?
Must I await the grand apocalypse alone,
While dear sister rests in laziness,
Listening to the dribblings of the Good Sir,
Waiting for current wisdom
While hopes for eternal life are abandoned?

Does she not know that God will have no slouchers,
No fat sow sitting at her garbage trough?
Does she not recognize that the grand Creator
Wishes to create,
To get on with His business—
And will listen to no man?
So, why should she sit and listen,
When busy-ness of service is at hand?

Instead, what does she?
An ignorant wretch, idly listening—
And where is the One to teach her?
This Good Sir!

Should not this Good Sir mention,
(Softly, if he pleases)
That she earns nothing listening to his tales
And wagging tongue—
All of his religiosity—
And answers to the universal riddles?
Should not the Good Sir pause one moment
To set this maiden on the trek to righteousness?
Is he not doing her a disfavor
By remaining silent on this most important issue?

Should not this Good Sir
Softly bespeak his wisdom concerning priority?
Should he not have her come to help the struggling—
Her own sister, no less—
The one who is in great need of help—
The one who wishes to please this Good Sir,
From whom wise droplets of phraseology echo in the mind?

It *is* a matter of priority:
Whether to help serve the Good Sir,
Or to sit idly by at his feet,
Helplessly doing naught.
Which is it? Which should it be?
Ah, for me there is no decision;
One must serve while service is due.

And, at that conclusion, I cried aloud, enraged,

> Please, Sir, is it not enough injustice
> That I should have to work slavingly
> While my dear sister sits idly by?
> Will you not do *your* part
> By explaining to her this matter of priorities?
> Can you not offer some excellent words,
> Enlightening her mind,
> So that she, too, knows
> That her priorities should be set
> In *service* to you, Good Sir,
> And not, as is now evident to me,
> In sitting wastefully by,
> Netting your jeweled words?
> Will you not, Good Sir,
> Tell her that her priorities are a bit confused,
> If nothing more?

And he, kind-eyed and lovingly,
Bespoke softly, addressing
This poor confused wench—
Addressing me, not my sister—
Addressing *me,* the one
With the clear priorities—
Addressing *me,* fallen-countenanced,
Inquiringly confused—
Addressing *me,* saying,

> Martha, Martha, your anxiety is evident.
> You are distracted about small things.
> Your heart is wrongly placed.
> Martha, good lady,
> You have decided that your *service* is best,
> And (while greatly appreciated) has met its test—
> You are right in questioning priorities,
> But can you not understand
> That your priorities are out of hand?

You put first what must be last.

Many things there are, dear lady,
About which priorities must be set—
Your list is no doubt long—
But confusion has run rampant in its midst;
You have put first what must be last,
And left the best until the end.

Nay, dear lady,
Sister Mary has chosen best.

With that, he turned again to Sis,
And began again to teach her this
High truth, now brought down to me—
Of utmost priority is *He*
And all his presence, mightily here
Embodied.

Oh, are not clothes important?
And is not the food we eat of prime necessity?
But which is our priority?

And I think back,
Where once the Master said,
Teaching from the hillside—
   Do not worry in your heart
   Concerning food or clothes or anything comfortable.
   Instead, it is your duty to give first place
   To your Father's kingdom,
   And all these necessities will be added to you.

And did he not also pronounce,
Extemporaneously exclaiming
That grand sentence:

   Save not for yourselves treasures on earth,
   Where moth and rust consume,
   And thieves break in and steal.
   Rather, save up for yourselves some treasures in heaven—
   For where your heart is,
   There will your treasure be, too.

Is not one able to discover where her treasure is
By first discovering where her heart is?

Oh, Martha, Martha,
Where is your heart?
Is your treasure in mundanity,
In keeping up with small details?
Should not your troubled heart
Be set more upon heavenly priorities?

Yet it matters not concerning heavenly priorities here.
My concern lies in priorities
To be set right now.
Must I keep my same list

With all its worldly trappings?
Am I to give first place
To these clankering kitchen utensils,
To all the pretty glitter
That the world has to offer?
Or is my first priority to be heaven-sent *love,*
To give people *me*
And not my worldly gourmet delights?

Have I my priorities straight?
Do I spend everything recklessly
(Since there are no pockets in a shroud),
To use and abuse the way I like
During this earthly existence?

Yet heaven-bound treasures are
True determinants to life today,
Valid priority-setting devices.
And where is your heart, Martha?
Is it caught up in worldly dealings?
Or is it bound up in a heavenly harness?
Is my proper priority
To keep my eyes heavenward,
To seek what the grand Creator has for me?
Is my priority plainly to serve the Good Sir,
Or to serve me?

These thoughts scampered through my troubled mind,
And, knowing well the answers true,
I began a rearrangement of priorities
By leaving behind my pots and pans and pantry room,
And taking my place at the feet
Of the Good Sir.

7 Narratives in Series

As in any regular preaching schedule where sermons are offered in series, so the narrative can also be used effectively in this manner. Any time may be right for such a series. Any usual theme for a series is conducive to narrative use. However, perhaps the most faithful times for narratives in series is during the Advent or Lenten seasons.

In a series of narratives three approaches are possible.

1. The points of view should be varied, along with types of characterizations (biblical, nonbiblical, historical, or contemporary).

2. The intent or written purpose of each of the narratives may be several facets of one single theme. Thus narratives would be tied together thematically but not in any other way.

3. As another possible series method, each week a different character could tell his or her side of one story. Again, purpose would vary according to point of view, and it would be wise to choose a Scripture passage that has the possibility of different perspectives and purposes.

Included in this chapter is one Lenten series preached over the course of three weeks. The narratives were given in the following order:

"Andrew" was given two weeks before Easter on a Communion Sunday.

"A Pharisee" was preached on Palm Sunday.

During our Maundy Thursday Communion service, the "Cross-Maker" told his story.

"Simon of Cyrene" was given at a community Good Friday worship.

Finally, on Easter Sunday morning, "Joseph of Arimathea" shared the power of the resurrection.

My intent in presenting these narratives was to look at the Passion story from different points of view:

Andrew, a biblical believer;

A Pharisee, a nonbiblical nonbeliever;

the Cross-Maker, a nonbiblical believer;

Simon of Cyrene, a repentant believer; and

Joseph of Arimathea, an ashamed follower of Jesus.

Andrew

Scripture: 1 Corinthians 11:23-26
Purpose: The remembrance of Communion
Costume: Robe

I am Andrew. I come from a family of fishers, and I had always loved the fishing business. I loved even more the things of God. My elder brother, Simon, and I got along quite well, except that he was headstrong and would run into things sometimes—get himself in trouble, if you know what I mean.

When I was a young man, I heard of a prophet called John, a baptizer out in the wilderness. He preached repentance and a baptism of cleansing. Well, I listened to John and what he had to say and realized that I needed to repent. So I did and was baptized by John in the Jordan and became a disciple of his, and we looked for the coming Messiah. That's what John told us.

One day John pointed to a man who had come out to be with us, and he said, "There is the Lamb of God." And after some bit of thought, Philip and I (Philip is a boyhood friend from Bethsaida where we grew up) went with that Lamb of God. When he asked us what we were looking for, we asked him where he lived. He showed us, but when Philip saw the shack, he left. He thought the Messiah would live in a better place than that.

Well, I went and got Simon and brought him to this new friend. His name, incidently, was Jesus, and the minute Jesus saw Simon he renamed him Peter, which means Rock. I suppose Jesus meant that Simon had character like a rock. I thought Simon's head was like a rock.

Anyway, the next day we saw Philip again, and Jesus asked him if he would like to follow him. So Philip, seeing that I had convinced Simon to join up, too, decided that it might be OK; so he went and got another guy named Nathanael. Nathanael was a real thinker and meditated a lot.

Philip and I were pretty good friends. We stuck together quite a bit during the next three years, as we had when we were disciples of John. Philip and I got along quite well because he didn't have a lot of faith, and I would always strengthen his faith by trusting Jesus. Sometimes it would be blindly, but I knew somehow that Jesus would take care of any problem situations.

For instance, once there was a pretty good-sized crowd that was following Jesus, and Jesus was teaching them. Well, it got sort of late in the afternoon, and Philip and I thought that we had better disperse this crowd since they were hungry and so were we. We went to Jesus, and Philip told him that we had better send the people away—perhaps to farmhouses or villages in the area. Jesus asked us how much food we had. So we went to look. (It would have taken about two hundred dollars worth to feed all this crowd— there were over five thousand people there at least). After searching for a few minutes, I could only find one young boy with a sack lunch.

Now to tell you the truth, I didn't think that was any big deal, but as I said, Philip was with me, and sometimes he needed a small demonstration of faith; so I took the lad with me to Jesus and said, "Jesus, here's a little lad who has a sack lunch—ah, five pieces of barley bread and a couple of fishes. I don't know what good they are, but that's all I could find among the crowd."

Well, Jesus put his hand on the boy's shoulder and told us to ask the people to sit down in groups on the grass, which we did. Then in the stillness, as if the people were expecting something great—even the birds stopped chirping—we could almost hear the wind whistle across our faces. Jesus looked up to heaven and said grace for the little boy's lunch; then he broke the barley bread and fishes and gave them to us to pass out. Now I don't know what went on then, but something strange sure happened! There was enough bread to go around and fish, too; and everybody ate and we had a great time eating outdoors there on the grass, laughing together. Some children were playing tag, and we were having the greatest time. And then Jesus told us to get some baskets and pick up the extra food, which we did, and gathered twelve full baskets of leftovers. Jesus didn't want anything to be wasted.

When it suddenly dawned on us what had happened, we were dumbfounded. I guess sometimes it pays to take a chance with Jesus. He took what little faith I displayed and made a pretty big deal out of it.

Well, it seems that the people wanted to make Jesus a king

right after they had their supper, but Jesus didn't want any part of it. He told us to disperse the crowd, and then he went up into the hills to pray and be by himself. Those of us who were his Twelve got in a boat and headed across the lake. It was the next day that the people apparently got wind that Jesus was over there now; so they flocked around the lake and met up with us. And that's when Jesus told them that he was the "bread of life." That's right. He went into a long speech about how bread was necessary to life and he himself was the bread of life—that without him a person can't really live.

To tell you the truth, I can't remember every word that he said, but it made an impact on me and, I guess, on the crowd. A lot of people decided to follow Jesus that day. And now every time I break bread, I think of that picnic time, and how Jesus used five pieces of barley bread to feed such a large crowd, and how Jesus said he was the bread of life. But that's not all. That time that Jesus fed all those people always reminds me of the last supper that we had with Jesus—it was a Passover meal that we shared down in Jerusalem. It was before the crucifixion.

I remember how my brother Simon and his friend John were told to go and get the meal ready. They would find a man carrying a water jar (strange thing—a *man* carrying a water jar) and were to follow him and find an upper room—guest room on the roof of a friend's house—and that we'd meet them there later on in the day.

It was a nice room, though plain (as are most roof rooms). It had been set up with all the Passover fixings. The people who owned the house had prepared the meal for us, and one of the members of the family served us the various courses.

We began the Passover remembrance (how the angel of death passed over the doors with lamb's blood on them). Jesus offered prayer and then said, "I won't eat this again until it has full meaning in the kingdom of God." There were lots of things that Jesus said that didn't mean too much to us at the time. That was one of them. I didn't know what he meant, but I quickly forgot about it when Jesus got up from his reclining position at the table and got a basin and towel and started to wash our feet. No one else had thought to do it, and when Simon asked Jesus not to wash his, Jesus said that he couldn't be one of his disciples. So Simon blurted out for Jesus to wash his head and hands, too. I thought that was a little dramatic, but it's true; Jesus shouldn't have been washing our feet.

We ought to have been washing his. But that's Jesus for you—always willing to give himself when we aren't willing to.

Then Jesus told us about how we ought to serve one another—according to the example that he had set. "The greatest among you," he said at one time, "will be the one who serves." That's hardly the way the world does things, but that's Jesus' way. Then Jesus said that we were all clean, except one. I thought he had washed everyone's feet, but I guess not.

Well, in the course of the meal, Jesus took that Passover bread from the table and said, "This is my body which is broken for you. Eat it in memory of me." Just like that he said it. That was another thing that didn't make much sense at the time, but I fully appreciate it now. He passed the bread around and we all ate it, a bit confused about what was going on, but we were pretty good boys.

Then we went ahead with the Passover remembrance. Jesus took the cup—the third or fourth, as I remember—and held it up in front of us and said, "Now this cup is God's new covenant, sealed with my blood. Drink it in memory of me." That was another strange thing that we didn't understand at the time, but we do now.

Then when the meal was almost over, Jesus started a big argument. He said, "One of you is going to betray me." Those are common words now, but that warm evening they stunned us like a bucket of cold water thrown on a man with a fever. You see, I had felt often that I was not worthy. I thought about times when I didn't really want to follow Jesus any longer. I thought about times when I didn't . . . but that's just it—I didn't want. But I had committed my life to Jesus and to his life-style and had committed myself to follow his teachings.

Sure, I thought I could probably betray him. But I was ashamed of it. I knew that I didn't really want to do it. I didn't want to let him down. He was so good to us. He taught us about love.

"Is it me, Lord?" I asked. I guess everyone of us at the table asked the same question, but Jesus never really answered us. Judas left to pay the provider of the meal—he carried our money pouch for us. Then we sang our closing hymn and went out to go to the garden.

It was a warm evening, and it took us half an hour or so to get to Gethsemane. Well, after that meal and the confusion and the warm night air and the walk, I got a bit sleepy. Some of us curled up on a soft spot of ground in the garden. Jesus oftentimes would pray all night, and I wasn't ready for that this night, especially because I seemed so tired.

The next thing I knew was Jesus shouting in my ear, "Get up! Let's go. Here comes the man who is betraying me." I shook my head quickly and jumped to my feet. Standing at the gate to the garden there was a mob of men with several flickering torches, Judas standing with them. "So, Judas is the betrayer," I thought. Judas walked up to Jesus and kissed him. The mob followed; Simon quickly drew his sword and hacked at one of the men. "This is it," I thought. "The end has come. We'll all perish here in the garden. My life has come to its close. This is it—all for nothing. I could carry on Jesus' work elsewhere." My head began to swim. My stomach felt nauseous. I was about to faint, and one of the soldiers was coming at me. I turned and ran, ran fast as I could, leaped the garden fence and ran back into Jerusalem. I had a cousin who lived in the city, and I headed to his house.

To be honest, I don't know firsthand all the events that followed. They apparently had dragged Jesus off to the high priest's house for a quick court session where they convicted him of blasphemy, and then rushed him to the governor's house, who didn't want to get his hands dirty in the deal. So he sent him off to Herod, but Herod only wanted to see a miracle; so he sent him back to Pilate who finally, I guess because of the crowd, handed Jesus over to be killed. I still can't understand why the good people get all the raw deals.

Simon told me some time later that Jesus had been beaten with short sticks by some of the soldiers, and they laughed at him, and he was given the scourging before he went to the cross. His back had been ripped open with the lash. And then he was made to carry his cross to the crucifixion hill. That was midmorning.

I had trouble sleeping that night, as you can imagine. The next morning I heard a mob coming down the street past my cousin's house. I looked out the window. And there along with two others (who looked like rough men) came Jesus, slowly, bleeding, some bramblesticks wrapped around his head, fainting. My heart wept.

I got up enough courage to go to Golgotha a bit later. I knew that I had to be with him. It looked like a storm was brewing up, and the wind was kicking up, and there was Jesus, stark naked with the two others, hanging, writhing in pain, slowly suffocating, half dead. It wasn't just my heart that wept now; I felt the tears well up in my eyes, and the dust made my nose drippy.

And Jesus looked up at the churning clouds and said, "Eli, Eli, lama sabacthani," which means, "My God, My God, why did you abandon me?" And it was as if he said to me, "Andrew, Andrew, why did *you* abandon me?"

And there were crowds. And friends and family of the crucified ones. And some who were curiosity seekers. There were always some sick people who were at all the crucifixions. And pretty soon Jesus said, almost in a whisper, "It is finished." And he slumped.

And then the earth moved. And some wind and dust blew in my eyes, and some women were sobbing, someone wailed aloud, and the earth kept trembling. I, too, knew that it was finished. I shall never ever forget that sight as long as I live.

I went to find Philip. He wasn't there at Golgotha—at least I hadn't seen him. Philip never did have a very good stomach. I wandered aimlessly around Jerusalem in the drenching rain, walking, looking for Philip as if he were the only friend I had left. I went back to the place where we had our supper the night before. Philip and Simon and Nathanael were there, not talking, just sitting in silence. When I came in, they looked up at me, then back at the floor. Simon was sniffling.

I decided I had better say something. I cleared my throat. "I remember last night. Jesus said that the bread was his body, broken for us. And the wine his blood. I didn't think he meant so soon though. Maybe we should pray." I got on my knees and waited. The others did, too, and we prayed together, sobbing, remembering, at a loss for words. With Jesus, praying was easy. But now he wasn't here. He taught us that God is love, and so I spilled my guts out in the sloppiest and most irreverent prayer I had ever prayed. Jesus was dead. How could God allow that to happen to Jesus, who thought he was God's only son?

When we were finished praying, the rain had stopped, and I went down the street to the synagogue services.

I guess we made fools out of ourselves those two days. Sulking, blubbering idiots, easily upset, quick to cry, moping around feeling sorry for ourselves. And our lack of sleep didn't help either.

And then on Sunday morning when we were together, the women came crashing into our meeting place saying that Jesus was alive. They had seen him. Peter and John took off. They knew where the tomb was and were headstrong anyway. There was a lot of confusion, and most of us just waited for them. But they came back soon and said it was just like the women said—the tomb was empty and the grave wrappings were lying there just as though the body had dematerialized through them.

And that night Jesus met with us, then was gone. And I saw Jesus two or three times after that. He would come and go quickly, but we knew he was alive, and our hope was not dead. And then he was taken up into heaven from us some time later.

Every time I eat this bread, I remember how Jesus died on the cross. I remember who I am and how much I have failed him. And I pledge to do better. And when I drink this cup, I think of Jesus' blood-stained body and his wounds and how he died for me. Every time I come to this table, I remember because there is so much to remember.

A Pharisee

Scripture: Luke 19:37-44
Purpose: Peace with God is ours through the personal love of Jesus
Costume: Robe and Pharisaic headdress

I had not thought there would be such a noise, such an uproar, such a cacophony of clatter. Those people ought to know better. One's tender ears can only take so much, and this noise pollution has gotten way out of hand. Is this crowd proud of itself, getting worked up to such a frenzy that its people have strewn their cloaks on the ground? And the children have gone and cut tree branches to wave in the air! Are they happy with their hoarseness now that they cannot shout any longer? Oh, crowds are so easily led. Go ahead and wave your palms loudly. What good will that do? This Carpenter will be dead before the week is out.

But even now that he has passed by, I can still hear the distant screaming and singing coming from over the hill, the unrighteous display of affection, the mob's shouting carried by the wind. He has gone now, down into the city over which he wept, the city in which he will die. And, furthermore, who is going to clean up this mess?

It was right there in the midst of the rowdy crowd when Jesus was approaching, that I and the others of our small delegation rushed up to Jesus. We had tried to quiet the people but to no avail. I touched the sleeve as I walked alongside him. "Teacher," I demanded, "tell your disciples to be quiet! They are making entirely too much noise! And they are making fools out of themselves."

And he merely turned to look at me, jostling along on the donkey, as if I had asked the impossible. In the midst of all the uproar he shouted, "If I told them to be quiet, then the stones would shout!" The stones? Ha! The man is a fool, a self-deluded prophet. He doesn't even have control of his own disciples. Some leader! Some king! Some Messiah!

It was because of that "Messiah" title that our small delegation of Pharisees has left the city, has come here to the Mount of Olives. We have heard rumors that this Carpenter, Jesus, is making a claim to messiahship, putting himself on par with God. We had heard that he was coming to town for the Passover celebration, and we wanted to meet him along the road to question him, perhaps to deter him from his purposes. And he came riding on a royal beast; and then this crowd, primarily pilgrims to Passover, reacted. Why had they come? Why pay such homage to this Jesus? Nothing good has ever come out of Nazareth. (And you certainly can't believe everything you hear about this teacher.) But these ignorant masses *do* believe, and we cannot do a thing about it. Just think of the things he's said about us, the religious leaders! He has always found something wrong with our life-styles, with our teachings, with the ways that we treat people. He *has* given the common people a bad impression of who we really are. They are shying away from us now, as if they distrust us.

But not all of us Pharisees are such scoundrels, and certainly not all of us are as pompous as Jesus would have the people believe. Take me, for instance. I am young, yes—but I am old in wisdom. I spend most of my day in prayer. I tithe (and more). I discuss the Law. I always have the things of God on my mind. I am not as bad as Jesus would have the people believe. That's why I came here—to set things right, to find out the real intentions of the Carpenter. I am not telling any secrets when I say that he has stirred up a good bit of controversy in our circles, and when we heard that he was coming here, we came to speak with him.

It's not often that I get out to this part of the city—to the Mount. But it has been a nice day, perhaps a bit cool from the wind, but I am used to the breezes from the open temple yard where I spend most of my time arguing the Law. I don't come out here much, I guess, because the roads are dusty and there is little shade from the glaring sun. When I do leave the city, I like to stroll alone. This road is well traveled, folks coming from Bethany and Bethphage into Jerusalem. And there have been so many travelers today, pilgrims coming to the Holy City for Passover. Many I have noted from the north, from Galilee, from where the Carpenter grew up, especially those in that unruly mob.

Now I pause, all alone, the crowds having gone with the

Carpenter. The other members of my committee have gone as well. I told them I would meet them in the temple yard later in the day, that I had some things to think through. As many Jerusalemites know, I am one of the foremost debaters concerning blasphemy and the Law. I have heard enough of this Jesus, this self-appointed Son of God about whom the crowds so indelicately shout. But the Law is to be upheld. And my specialty is blasphemy. Jesus has tricked us before with his cleverness, but this is his final outrage, his concluding act of blasphemy, his last move. He has demonstrated today his intentions. He has ridden into our city on a royal beast. He comes to conquer and to be king. And that is the Messiah's duty. And I know that a case can be made against him. There must be strict accuracy in the interpretation of the Law concerning blasphemy. He cannot escape from the Law.

Yet as I think, there are some of our number—some who are Pharisees—who have the greatest respect for Jesus. Nicodemus has been getting ideas about the Carpenter. I can tell by the way he acts in the presence of Jesus. Never anything spoken, however. That would be foolish. There are rumors and easily sensed under-rumblings, but nothing is brought out into the open.

I could expect more of a man of the Sanhedrin. But these crowds—they are ignorant. I expect nothing better from them. They just kept on shouting for Jesus, and my ears rang at the outrage. Here is a man with a mark on his head, who has been warned, and he enters the Holy City in broad daylight. Because I was schooled in the laws concerning blasphemy, this day's activities have only confirmed the rumors I have heard right along. The man comes riding as a king, and the people have been shouting, and he made no attempt to quiet them down, even after I had spoken to him about it.

Yes, the man angers me. He angers me in his tricks. He angers me in the ways that he misleads the people.

He angers me in his gentleness.

And he confuses me in his love.

The crowd had just kept on shouting and waving those palms after I had demanded that he quiet them down. I walked with him as he rode to the peak of the Mount, just where he could see the entire city and surroundings. He stopped and stared out across the golden city, and he took a great breath. I was stunned as he slumped forward on the animal and began to weep. Then he ran the back of his hand across his eye and sat up and just kept staring at the city. The "hosannas" of the crowd grew louder, and the skipping and dancing people were all about, joyful, and there sat their leader, their Messiah, weeping, staring. I thought at first that he knew that he was riding to his death.

But, no, he wasn't weeping for his death. And he wasn't crying for joy. (You can tell when a man sobs because people love him.) It seems, as I consider it, that the Carpenter was weeping as if his people didn't love him. He was just showing *his* love and how much he cared for the city.

And as he sat still, amidst the worshiping crowd, staring over the city, he said, almost so that no one heard him: "If only you knew what was needed for peace. But you can't see it. Your enemies will come and barricade you in and tear down your walls and not a single stone will be left in place. You will never know peace because you failed to recognize when God came to save you." I don't know if he was addressing the city or me.

Here was the self-appointed Messiah, *not* having come to save the city which was his prophesied duty, but here he was predicting its downfall. And he said that we would never know peace. I tell you that we will know peace because we Pharisees are doing something about it. We're scheming with the Romans in political arenas to vie for peace. There will be peace; you will see. But it will come through the efforts of those who are concerned about peace, not through some nobody who will be forgotten in a year's time.

But then, Jesus has equated peace with *God saving us*. Perhaps he is *not* speaking of political peace but *peace with God*. Ah, but that too is sheer nonsense. We have peace with God. We are the Chosen People, are we not? Peace comes through obedience to the Law, not in any man's relationship with God. I trust that the crowd doesn't really believe that. It is as if Jesus were to say that peace with God can only be achieved through him. And *that* is blasphemy. In spite of his love, I refuse to believe that.

Oh, but now the crowds are gone. The shouting has followed the Carpenter into the city. Those poor, misled people; they are worshiping a false teacher.

Or is he? I do not know. It is so difficult to imagine, to piece together, that the true Messiah could come in my lifetime. But this Jesus must die now, now that he has made his move by riding into the city. He will die before the Passover begins, at end of the week. I promise myself that. I will have it done. We had warned him to keep still, but now this public display will bring about his downfall. We must go to the ultimate lengths. I must speak to Caiaphas—or perhaps Annas—before nightfall.

But I am so uneasy. I am so unsure.

That picture still lingers: Jesus, weeping atop his beast, slumped over. The crowds, waving their palms loudly, raising their voices in praise. Jesus, realizing that the city has not believed in him after all, crying because all of God's people have not followed him. And he is right. I will not believe in him.

Yet I will always remember, fixed firmly in the back of my mind, Jesus sobbing, brushing aside the tears from his wet eyes, using the back of his hand. He had turned his head and looked right at *me,* his eyes red and swollen. It was then that I knew that he wasn't crying because he was going to his death, nor was he crying for the buildings and streets of Jerusalem, but he was crying for *me* because I would not give him my life, because I would not believe that he had come to bring peace with God. And I saw in his look that he could see me for who I am—just a fool—and I saw love, that he loved me though I wouldn't take that step of faith and follow him.

And I looked away, because his tears and his red, swollen eyes were for me, and I could not and will not believe. Perhaps he still weeps for me. Perhaps he still loves me, but I will have him dead before the week is out. I must do my duty.

The Cross-Maker

Scripture: Mark 15:15-20, 22-28, 33-37
Purpose: Jesus went through the agony of crucifixion because of his love
Prop: A carpenter's apron

I saw a lad this morning with a stick. He scratched a cross in the sand, and all around it he drew "glory lines" as if the cross was all lit up. I made the boy cry when I scuffed out that cross with my sandal. It turns my stomach, see, to make a cross a polished symbol that glitters in the light. They make 'em now with pretty designs, and some wear 'em around their necks as dangling symbols. You see, crosses just ain't like that. They ain't fine and polished. Crosses are crude and rough. They give you slivers, and they're used to kill men.

I ought to know what a cross is like. I used to make the bloody things. But I quit making 'em about a year ago. It was when I found out that they'd used one of my crosses to nail Jesus, the Carpenter, the appointed one from God. It didn't mean nothing to me at the time, but it was a couple of months later when the roughnecks started preaching about Jesus. I heard one of 'em, a big one called Peter, preaching one day. He said how this Jesus died on a cross, but he rose from the dead, and he died there to get us right with the Creator. I listened, because I knew I was the one who made that cross, and I believed in Jesus then, and I follow him now. He taught us about love, and there ain't no place in love for crosses.

Besides, I seen that Jesus once after he was dead—I mean, after he was alive. I seen the hole scars in his hands. He showed 'em to me. I wanted to get a good look at his back, just to make sure, but I never got a chance to ask him.

Crosses are cruel things. And nobody in his right mind would go to die on a cross. But Jesus did. And he didn't have to do it. But he did because he loves me—that's why he did it. He wasn't no criminal. He was a good guy. And Peter says that Jesus died there on the cross because he wanted me to get right with God. He died on the cross to forgive me for my sins. Jesus went there because I'm a downright scoundrel—there's no getting around that. When I look at my life set up against his, there ain't no comparison. Sometimes I wish I could have gone to the skull hill instead of him. I deserve it, but he sure didn't.

And now sometimes I get nightmares. I jerk awake at night, thinking about how many men I've killed on my crosses. But then, sitting up in the dark, I think about how Jesus took all that guilt away. And then I feel better, and I think that I'm sort of a hero of sorts, because if it wasn't for my cross, he never would have died, and I couldn't have the new life I got now. You see, you get new life when you follow the Carpenter, when you believe in him.

I want to tell you about crucifixions so's you'll know what Jesus did. You heard Peter and the others preach before, but you maybe never seen a crucifixion.

The Romans would commission me to do crosses for 'em— sometimes I'd get an order for twenty-five or thirty. I'd buy the timber, and I'd plane 'em down and would have to notch the pieces so they fit together, and I'd fasten 'em with wooden pegs. Them was the good crosses. They paid more for them. When there wasn't a big order, I'd make the good ones, but sometimes, when I had lots to make, I made the other ones where the crossbeam just sat on a peg on top of the upright. That was easier to do and didn't take so much time.

Then was the hard part, when the saddle had to get fitted on. That was a piece of four-by-six that was inserted in the upright, where the criminal sat. For crosses with saddles, I charged extra. That was a lot of work, gouging out a hole big enough to slip the four-by-six in, then secure it. Usually just a good soaking job would hold the saddle in place until it had served its purpose.

There were reasons for the saddle (there are always reasons that the Romans have for doing things). First off, the saddle helped hold the criminal when he was lifted. It saved him from tearing his hands. Then he'd sit on that seat, which prolonged the suffocation process, but it caused extra pain, too, the criminal being naked and all.

I remember Pilate used crosses a lot, but when they cut his budget, the cross business got a little slow. Then he started using some of the crosses over again. They only had to be washed down. Except some. There were some that were just too bad off, and they were burned.

Well, any time a criminal was going to get nailed, he got the scourging. That was so he'd die quicker. I've seen some guys die under the whip. They get this big soldier who comes with a whip of leather straps, and there's bits of bone or metal tied on the ends. Here in the Jews' country, they get it thirty-nine times. The criminal is stripped and bent over and gets two-thirds on his back and a third on his chest. The first flogging I seen, the guy died on the spot after twenty-two. That's no pretty picture, believe you me.

Peter says he watched the whole thing, and he told me that after Jesus got his whipping, he could hardly stand up, but the soldiers are typical Romans. They took Jesus and one of them propped him up and they stripped him all the way and brought a royal robe and put it on him and made a branch crown with thorns on it and had their fun laughing and hitting him on the head where the thorns were. You'd think they'd know better. They should have let the man die in dignity. Peter said they were still drunk from a party that lasted all the night before.

And they always make the criminal carry his own cross. The ones that got nailed in a big group were lucky—they only had to carry the crossbeam, but Jesus was one of three that morning, and I made the specials of the house—that's what I called 'em. I usually did my best work right around Passover time.

I heard that Jesus didn't make it all the way. Some thought he was going to die on the road. They always take you the long way around and out to the skull hill where they do the crucifixion. They tear off all the clothes and the soldiers get to keep the clothes, and the criminal is laid flat on the cross on the ground, on his back which was all tore up from the whipping, and he'd usually get slivers, the crosses being pretty crudely made, as I said. One of the soldiers held the guy's head and one of the others slapped his right arm out, and "thump, thump" just that quick the spike went in, and then the other side and they did the same on the feet. Then all four soldiers took the cross and lifted it up and dropped it into the cross hole with a thud.

Jesus never did anything to make them do that. But the lousy Romans nailed him. He was hanged there in hot sun, slowly suffocating, hanging off the saddle, then pushing himself back on. Later in the day they came around to break the legs so the man couldn't push himself up on the saddle anymore and that would hasten the suffocation, but they found Jesus dead already. Sometimes they'd even light fires underneath so the fumes would choke the man off, but with the storm and all, that couldn't be done. And besides, as I said, Jesus was already dead. It was raining by then, Peter said, and I remember he was right because we were almost ready to go over to the temple for the Passover festivities. The others who were crucified with Jesus weren't quite dead yet; so they broke their legs and they died shortly before nightfall.

And Jesus was taken by a friend and they put him in a borrowed grave, and then, like I said before, he rose up again first of that next week. And when we follow him and ask him into our lives, he makes us right with God and forgives our sins.

I gave up making crosses. Before it was a business. Now it's a personal thing. Crosses sure ain't no polished, dangling symbols. They're made to kill men on. And I know that Jesus died on one of my crosses so he could save me from dying. And when I faced up to him and believed in him, all my sins and guilt and hurt and selfishness were gone. Now I can live for him.

Every time I think of the cross, it upsets my stomach. I think of how great it was for Jesus to die on a cross for me because he loves me, and he proved it. When I think of that cross, I think about the torture, yes, but I also think about Jesus. And mostly I think about love, how much Jesus loves me and how much I love him.

Simon of Cyrene

Scripture: Luke 23:26-34a
Purpose: Jesus calls us to responsibility
Costume: Robe, headdress, and sandals

Sure, I remember. Who could forget? Besides, it was only a couple of years ago that it happened.

Cyrene is a nice little town, capital city, in fact, of Cyrenaica in North Africa. It wasn't that I wanted to leave or anything like that. The whole city is made up of Greek-speaking Jews, and a thing that we all looked forward to was a trip to the Holy City for Passover—a pilgrimage. There's always something spiritual and life-giving about a pilgrimage. Trouble is that it's about a thousand miles to Jerusalem, and folks in my walk of life can only make the trip once in a lifetime, if that. I had a rich uncle who had passed on and left me a bit of cash. I added that to my savings and decided that that was the year to go. That's why I got to go while still pretty young. Three others from our synagogue went that year, and we had a great time. I left the wife and my two boys, Rufus and Alexander, at home. They were provided for easily enough. I had pinched pennies for years just for this one trip to Jerusalem, and with the windfall of Uncle Ephraim, I knew I could make the trip and stay at the best inn, too.

Well, we got to Jerusalem at last, and checked in to the best inn in town, across the city from the temple, but we were there a couple of days early so we could get in some sight-seeing. After all, this is the Holy City.

Passover is such a special celebration when all the family meets together, but there's just something else about having it in the city, if you know what I mean. Something intangible. Oh, I missed celebrating with my family, but Jerusalem—you can't do any better than that.

It was on the morning of the Passover feast that I was out checking some of the little shops in the north part of the city. Traveling men ought always to bring something home to their boys and wife. I was in a textile store, I remember, when I heard some distant shouting, some uproar. I thought nothing of it at first and went back to check some of the yard goods, but the noise got increasingly louder. It was coming this way, and I stepped out on the street and could hear a crowd coming round the corner. There were children running on ahead with sticks and some angry men and others who were there for the sport of the thing. And suddenly it struck me that this was a crucifixion.

I had heard of crucifixions before. The Romans were unjustly cruel in their punishments, and I had heard that they took the dead bodies from the crosses and would throw them on the ground for the vultures and wild dogs. It wouldn't be that bad here, I thought, because this was a Jewish town, and that was against our Law.

I didn't want to have anything to do with this, and I almost turned to disappear back into the shop when something caught my eye. A little placard poked its trembling head around the corner. Through the crowd, I could see that it was carried by a soldier. Then came the criminal. He was surrounded by four soldiers, marching regularly, one out in front carrying a sign that I couldn't read at first because of the people; but when I saw it, it said, "King of the Jews," carried so that everybody could know who this was. Now I had not heard that we had a king; so I waited to get a better look at him. One of the soldiers had a whip to goad the prisoner on, to keep him moving. I heard a whip snap and saw the criminal fall only a half block from where I was standing. The cross that he was carrying fell heavily against his head, and he just lay there and then struggled to try to get up. I noted that behind him there were two more criminals, each with four soldiers, one in front carrying the placard. I was just trying to make out what those signs said when I saw one of the soldiers, not the one with the sign, coming toward me from the first man's group. He marched right up to me; I stuck out my hand: "Simon," I said, "Simon of Cyrene in northern Afric. . . ." I felt the slap of the flat of his spear on my shoulder. I was being called into service. I could tell the soldier wasn't interested in my name or where I was from by the way he grabbed me by the arm and gave me a shove toward the fallen man. I knew by this time that one doesn't argue with a Roman soldier.

I can still feel the steady pressure on my arm as that Roman guided me toward the prisoner lying on the ground. He had collapsed. A thousand thoughts raced through my head. Would they crucify me instead if this man died? Did they have to go through with it just to have a crucifixion? I tried to break away, but the soldier's grip was too firm.

I looked down at the man and at the enormous cross that he was carrying.

"The cross," I heard the guard say. "Pick it up." That was all, just "The cross—pick it up." And I did. It was a heavy cross, well made. As I lifted it from the dying man, I saw that he was still alive. He looked up at me, his face bruised and gritty from the fall. There was dried blood on his cheek, and under his robe, on his back, there was dirt and blood and I almost got sick, but I shouldered the cross and followed the soldiers slowly, too slowly.

The cross was hard to balance, and the bottom dragged on the ground and that held me up a bit.

The criminal had risen and was staggering along in front of me. I felt very odd being at the center of attention. I didn't want anyone to think that I was a criminal or even that I was "King of the Jews." But when pressed into service by the Romans, you do what you have to. And for that I hated the Romans, and those guards, and that criminal walking ahead of me. I had saved and scrimped to make a holy pilgrimage to the Holy City, and I was imposed upon in the cruelest way possible. I remember asking God what was going on, why this should happen to me. I was a good Jew.

We took the long way around. I'm not that familiar with Jerusalem, but I know that we were circling back and forth, and we picked up people as we went along. Almost on every corner there were angry men because of the placard. And at one point I was told to stop for a moment. This prisoner had stopped to talk with some women. He's going to his crucifixion, and I'm lugging his cross along, and he has to stop and chat with some women. I couldn't imagine the gall of that man, and the cross was getting heavy, what with all the lugging and dragging and its digging into my shoulder.

Well, we got moving again (one of the guards gave the man a little push—I think he was a little soft on the criminal). Finally, we left the city and headed up to a little rock hillside outside Herod's Gate—between there and the Damascus Gate. With a great deal of effort I was able to drag the cross over the stones and up the incline, and I was never happier in my life than to set that burden down. I stretched my aching muscles and had every intention of leaving the premises. The last thing I wanted was to watch a crucifixion during Passover season.

But I was caught again. I saw them rip the clothes off the man and throw him back against the rough cross. They offered him a drug, but he wouldn't take it. And with the quickness of regimentation one held his head while another pounded the spikes in his hands, then feet, and I watched while the cross was lifted (it took all four soldiers, and they were very efficient), and it dropped with a thud in the hole there, and the naked body of the criminal shuddered. But there was something intriguing about this man. He wasn't any ordinary criminal. He wasn't cursing as were the others. He didn't mind all the insults and crude jokes that were hurled up at him. And the sign was nailed above his head, there on the cross.

It said, "King of the Jews." *Some king,* I thought. Some king. It was gruesome.

And a storm started to kick up, and I wanted to leave, but there were so many fascinating things about this man that I was compelled to stay. When he caught my eye, he gave me a weak smile, and there was a tear in the corner of his eye. I just sat down on the ground.

I stayed a long while. The dust was kicking up, and storm clouds were brewing. This king of the Jews fascinated me. I began to ask what he got nailed for. I learned his name was Jesus, from Nazareth up in Galilee. And as I watched this Jesus, my hatred for the Romans grew stronger, and for this whole crucifixion business, but I suddenly realized that I had nothing against this man, that he would have been a good friend to know. They wanted to give him a drug to kill the pain again, but he wouldn't take it. And pretty soon, midafternoon, the man shouted and died. And one of the Roman guards was standing there, and he said, "Surely, this man *was* the Son of God." And then the earth trembled, and I went back to my inn. I packed my belongings and left for home on that very day. I couldn't stomach the Passover or the Holy City any longer. My pilgrimage was ruined.

It was a few months later, after severe nightmares of that holiday in Jerusalem, that a couple of fellows came to Cyrene preaching about a Jesus crucified and risen again.

I learned that he had been laid in a tomb and rose from the dead on the first day of the next week and did it all to bring us new life.

Well, that Jesus impressed me the way he smiled at me, tear in the corner of his eye, and somehow I knew that this was the one whom Jews had been waiting for for centuries—the Promised One, the Messiah, the Son of God—really, the King of the Jews. I believed in him, and just like I carried his cross that day, now I have to carry on his teaching and work. Come to my house sometime. I'd like to tell you more of what I learned about Jesus, the Son of God, the one who died and rose again, and that he died for you, brother, and about how he can give you new life, too.

No, I won't ever forget my pilgrimage or my love for Jesus.

Joseph of Arimathea

Scripture: John 19:38–20:10
Purpose: The resurrection power of Jesus enables one to be a public follower
Costume: Robe and judge's headdress, white beard

Nicodemus and I sat there amidst the swirling sand on that small rock ledge just outside Herod's Gate, looking up at Golgotha. There were three crosses. The sky was getting darker, and old Nicodemus and I were feeling sorry for ourselves. We had not put in a good word for the rabbi who was nailed upon the centermost cross. And well we could have. And well we should have.

Oh, we were followers in secret of the rabbi, Jesus of Galilee. He was just a youngster, but hearty and truthful, and when he spoke, he spoke *to* people, not over their heads as we Pharisees were taught to do. I admired him, that Jesus, but I admired him quietly, and it was my own secret. I was respected. When one has respect, one must not rock any boat. Respect is such a fleeting thing. One can never be too careful with one's reputation. Except, those were *my* values. Jesus could care less. He rubbed shoulders with all the sinners. And that irked the Sanhedrin and most of the Pharisees. But I admired Jesus for that. He was young and virile, and was filled with love overflowing, as an artesian well is constantly bubbling up its waters. And Jesus preached about bringing in the kingdom.

But that past week Jesus had gotten himself into hot water. He had finally roused the ire of members of the Sanhedrin to such a feverish pitch that Nicodemus and I knew that the young rabbi would die. We had not known that it would be so soon, but we did know that he was doomed. We, Nicodemus and I, were the only two secret admirers of Jesus on the Sanhedrin that we knew of. One is not open about those things when one's reputation is on the line. Since we knew he would die, Nicodemus and I planned to provide a decent burial for Jesus—I would give up my new tomb in my quiet garden. Nicodemus would provide the spices and ointments and shroud.

And it was very early that morning when Jesus had been brought before the Sanhedrin—an illegal meeting—yet when the crowd is furious, it has no patience. I was roused early enough to attend the session. Nicodemus was not. Some in the Sanhedrin suspected Nicodemus of being a follower of this Jesus, and they wanted no indecision. I have been more cautious, and no one knows that I follow Jesus. It is best that way. I have learned to keep my mouth shut and, thus, to save my honor, my pride, and my neck.

We met for several hours that morning before dawn to try to convict this Jesus of some crime worthy of death. At last two came forward with a blasphemy charge—their stories agreed somewhat— though a shrewd lawyer could have punched holes in their arguments large enough to drive a camel train through. *No one* spoke up on Jesus' behalf, and Caiaphas (mere puppet in the hands of Annas) tore his hem and shouted, "Blasphemy"—the act of a child—and we took a vote. I was helpless. I abstained from voting. It was unanimous. It was a time when Jesus needed a friend, and I had *not* the courage to offer that friendship. And after the vote Jesus, sadly, turned and looked at me—just a fleeting glimpse that cut me to the quick—just before they shoved him out of the chambers to take him to Pilate's headquarters, where they finally convinced Pilate to crucify this gentle teacher as a common criminal.

At that point Jesus was handed over for the flagellum—the thirty-nine lashes of leather and metal, and after that scourging, they made him carry his own cross (as was customary). He was weak, too weak, and he fell beneath the load of the timbers, and apparently a foreigner was called upon by the garrison to carry that cross the rest of the way. I had gone immediately to rouse my good friend, Nicodemus, and as he is aged (early seventies, I believe), it took him a while to dress himself. About noontime we came to Golgotha, where we sat on the rock ledge beside Herod's Gate, and we could see, against a steadily darkening sky, three forms nailed on crosses. I left Nicodemus there and went on up the hill to discern which was the Master, and I saw him in agony, half-dead, bleeding, hanging limply, with a crude sign over his head, "King of the Jews." And as I stood watching him, I examined myself. *I* could have spoken a word in his behalf; yet I was too concerned about my pride and reputation, and *I* was the guilty one. *I* was the one who was solely responsible for Jesus hanging there, naked, gasping for breath. And I went back, slowly, to where Nicodemus was sitting. And I sat. And the wind was kicking up the sand. I said, "He is on the centermost, Nicodemus," and took a deep breath to keep from sobbing. And Nicodemus laid one of his old, bony hands on my shoulder, and we sat there in silence.

It was midafternoon after the sky had gone dark for some time that the wind began to swell. The three crosses were just barely visible against the purplish backdrop, and we heard a loud cry and the body on the center cross hung heavily, and I looked at Nicodemus, and we knew that our friend, our secret friend, had died.

It started to rain, and there was thunder, and as we got to our feet, the earth rocked, and Nicodemus lost his balance and fell. But we regained our stature and knew that this was the time to act. I would go to Pilate and ask for the body. Nicodemus would go to buy spices.

I had no fear as I went to Pilate. Had anyone questioned me of my motives in caring for the blasphemer, I would have appealed to the Law, since no body was to be left unburied beyond the day of death. And since Jesus was from Galilee, he would have no family to claim the body, and I could say that I was a follower and could lay claim to it.

Pilate consented almost immediately. His senior officer was back from the day's crucifixion, and he asked him how long Jesus had been dead. "About half an hour," he said quietly, with a note of regret. "We broke the legs of the others, but the Galilean was dead. I gave him my spear tip just to see. He emptied blood and water. He is dead." Pilate said to him, "Go with this man. He claims the body of the King of the Jews." He rather sneered at me. But the senior officer and I climbed back up the hill where two of my servants met me with linen and candles, and the captain ordered the other soldiers to take down the Galilean. They did, and laid him on the ground, and my servants and I lifted the corpse. He was bruised. His hair was matted. His back a mass of ripped flesh and slivers from the cross and dirt. His skin was cold.

The body was unusually heavy. The three of us struggled with it down the hill to my garden, only a short distance, and we laid it outside on the ground. The fragrance in the garden almost over-whelmed me. There was beauty there that I had not noted before. It is strange how, in the midst of sorrow and death and pain, you notice things taken for granted—things that suddenly have rich meaning. But the fragrance of that heavy garden was not enough to soothe over the stench of death. And the death of a good man smells worse.

The servants went inside the tomb to prepare it, and they lit the candles, and we carried Jesus inside and they began to wash him. I went outside and sat down and waited for Nicodemus. It was still fairly dark, about four o'clock, but the rain had stopped. There were women behind the bushes there, weeping silently, and one of them became hysterical, and the others led her away.

It was approaching Sabbath. The body had to be finished by six o'clock. Shortly, Nicodemus came shuffling along with his two servants, each carrying large packages of spices and ointments. Nicodemus said, "One hundred pounds' worth of the best. The man had lived a pauper's life, but we shall give him a rich man's tomb and a king's burial." I nodded, though the weight of guilt still hung heavily upon my back. If only I had spoken up for the Master, bringer of the kingdom.

My servants came out. They had finished washing the body. Nicodemus and I went in and began the long process of wrapping and packing and filling and anointing, round and round. It took us a good hour to finish. The wrapping is tedious work and heavy work, but we did what I thought to be an excellent job. "Nothing but the best for the Master," Nicodemus said. When we had completed it, we straightened the folds and adjusted the body, now one hundred pounds heavier from the spices and ointments, and we laid the linen napkin over his face, softly, and went outside. The six of us rocked the giant stone until we moved it into place in the groove to seal up the tomb.

We sent the servants on ahead. And Nicodemus and I sat, alone, under the great olive tree. It was twilight, and the moon shone through, and we wept together. And we prayed for the memory of this man who was a secret friend. I asked God over and over again if I couldn't have just another chance. I felt empty and hollow, as if there were now no meaning to life. We did not feel like celebrating Passover, but knew that it was our duty to take part in the festivities. But then Nicodemus reminded me that we could not do that because we were ritually unclean now, having handled a body, and I was thankful and went to my home and spent the night, sleepless, tossing and turning and praying.

A day later it was early, just after dawn, that my gardener came pounding on my door, breathless. I snatched my robe and flung it around my shoulders and went sluggishly to the door. And he told me that the tomb had been broken into, that the body was gone, except for the linen wrappings that were lying there as if there was a body still in 'em, and some women had come down there, bringing more spices and ointment and they got hysterical and rushed off and shortly some big men came rushing down and he thought he had better come and tell me.

I hastily dressed and rushed to Nicodemus, who lives on the street called Narrow, and together, as fast as Nicodemus could dress, we hastened to my garden and my tomb. And the huge stone had been rolled back, and there was no one there except the gardener, and inside, just like he had said, the graveclothes were lying there as if the body had passed through them. They had not been tampered with. I was dumbfounded, and my heart was racing. I looked at Nicodemus and he was grinning, a toothless old grin. I smiled and slapped him on the back and we began to laugh until the tears were streaming down our faces.

Jesus was alive. We knew he was alive, had somehow come

back to life, because of the evidence of the graveclothes. God must have honored his self-sacrifice and raised him from the dead. And suddenly it dawned on me that I was filled. My life had been changed in that very instant of realization. All my guilt had gone. The Suffering Servant had died to forgive my guilt. And it had vanished and I could stand straight.

Both of us, Nicodemus and I, went to find the followers of Jesus, to see if there was anything we could do. Some of them had seen the Master, they said—he really was alive—and we knew now that there was a ministry and a kingdom to carry on. With un-characteristic abandon, we thumbed our noses at the Sanhedrin and at wealth and at fame and at pride, and turned that day to be open followers of Jesus—the Master, the Messiah, the Son of God, yes, the Son of God, and that is not blasphemy. I have new power to live because of that resurrection. This joy, this peace with God, this new life—I have been changed because of that morning, because the Risen One has changed it. *Jesus alive* is an experience, and he can be your experience, if you give him a chance. He can change your life, too. It doesn't matter your age or your priorities or your life-style.

When I realized that he died for me, that he removed my guilt, that he gave me peace with God and a new life, then I understood how much I had been missing in life. He died for me, and I know he died for you—and his resurrection has brought me that second chance to serve him, to speak up for him, to be an unashamed follower of his. I have joy and power now to live. And he could not give me that power for living if it weren't for that morning. And he cannot give you that power to live unless you ask him to.

That resurrection morning—what a morning that was!

Annotated Bibliography

Barclay, William, *The Master's Men*. Nashville: Abingdon Press, 1959.

A background study of the twelve apostles, but not in narrative style. Barclay deals with biblical information and legends about these characters and, in typical fashion, treats the matter with scholastic excellence.

Brownrigg, Ronald, *Who's Who in the New Testament*. New York: Holt, Rinehart & Winston, 1971.

Here is an excellent study guide for New Testament characters, complete with history and biblical references. A good reference tool.

Comay, Joan, *Who's Who in the Old Testament*. New York: Holt, Rinehart & Winston, 1971.

A companion volume to *Who's Who in the New Testament*. A fine reference addition for the narrative preacher.

Cornell, George W., *They Knew Jesus*. New York: William Morrow & Co., Inc., 1957.

These are short stories of New Testament characters. Well written, these third-person tales take one into the minds of biblical personalities.

Hager, Wesley, *They Were There*. Grand Rapids, Mich.: Wm. B. Eerdmans Publishing Company, 1966.

This is an unusual collection, consisting of many different types of narratives dealing with different topics. These are excellent presentations.

Hill, David C., *These Met the Master*. Minneapolis: Augsburg Publishing House, 1967.

Brief, poetic snatches of forty persons who encountered Jesus.

Good for inspiration and point-of-view studies. They are excellently done.

Hubbard, David Allen, *They Met Jesus*. Philadelphia: A. J. Holman Company, 1976.
A series of eleven narrative sermons used on the radio. Some have good background material included.

Kossoff, David, *The Book of Witnesses*. New York: St. Martin's Press, Inc., 1971.
Excellently written short narratives. Basically, these are non-biblical personalities telling the biblical stories. Good character description of these eyewitnesses. This book is especially helpful in developing creativity and insight into character traits.

Reid, John Calvin, *We Knew Jesus*. Grand Rapids, Mich.: Wm. B. Eerdmans Publishing Company, 1954.
A series of unusual narratives which are voices from the Beyond speaking to today's people. There is frequent use of contemporary poets and preachers, and most are quite creative presentations.

_____, *Why We Wrote the Gospels*. Grand Rapids, Mich.: Wm. B. Eerdmans Publishing Company, 1960.
These four narratives are from the Four Evangelists and are very nicely presented to include much background material and the unique approaches of each of the Gospel writers.

Speakman, Frederick, *Love Is Something You Do*. Old Tappan, N.J.: Fleming H. Revell Company, 1959.
This collection of sermons contains many narratives which are inspiring, challenging, and beautifully written.

Ward, J. W. G., *The Glorious Galilean*. Nashville: Abingdon Press, 1936.
A series of character studies on New Testament personalities. These are good narratives but are not preaching narratives.

_____, *The Master and the Twelve*. New York: George Doran Co., 1924.
Excellent background material with Scripture, quotations, and poetry included. These are good studies, though some of the language and presentation are outdated.

Weatherhead, Leslie, *Personalities of the Passion*. Nashville: Abingdon Press, 1943.
Third-person discussions of personalities surrounding the crucifixion of Jesus. These are well done, interesting presentations.